D0436758

THE ESSENTIAL
LINCOLN

THE ESSENTIAL
LINCOLN

SPEECHES AND CORRESPONDENCE

EDITED AND WITH AN INTRODUCTION BY

ORVILLE VERNON BURTON

HILL AND WANG

A DIVISION OF FARRAR, STRAUS AND GIROUX

NEW YORK

Hill and Wang
A division of Farrar, Straus and Giroux
18 West 18th Street, New York 10011

Copyright © 2009 by Orville Vernon Burton
All rights reserved
Distributed in Canada by Douglas & McIntyre Ltd.
Printed in the United States of America
First edition, 2009

Library of Congress Cataloging-in-Publication Data
Lincoln, Abraham, 1809–1865.
    The essential Lincoln : speeches and correspondence / edited and
with an introduction by Orville Vernon Burton.— 1st ed.
        p.   cm.
    Includes bibliographical references.
    ISBN-13: 978-0-8090-4307-1 (hardcover : alk. paper)
    ISBN-10: 0-8090-4307-6 (hardcover : alk. paper)
    1. Lincoln, Abraham, 1809–1865—Political and social views.
2. Lincoln, Abraham, 1809–1865—Oratory.   3. Lincoln, Abraham,
1809–1865—Correspondence.   4. United States—Politics and
government—1815–1861.   5. United States—Politics and government—
1861–1865.   6. Speeches, addresses, etc., American.   I. Burton, Orville
Vernon.   II. Title.

E457.92 2009c
973.7092–dc22

                                                    2009007734

Designed by Jonathan D. Lippincott

www.fsgbooks.com

1   3   5   7   9   10   8   6   4   2

*Frontispiece: Last photographic portrait of Abraham Lincoln,
by Alexander Gardner, Meserve Collection, courtesy of the Library of Congress*

I appreciate the suggestions and comments of Georganne Burton, David Herr, Doug Lippman, Stacy McDermott, Lewie Reece, and Chris Waldrep. As always, my publisher, Thomas LeBien, provided invaluable advice. This book is dedicated to my best friend, Bill Whitmire, who, like Lincoln, has made the world a better place.

For consistency and clarity, Lincoln's spelling and punctuation have been corrected and modernized.

Contents

Introduction

Among the many thousands of Lincoln's writings, published and unpublished, how does one choose the *essential* Lincoln? These writings were selected because they articulate Lincoln's vision of America, one of preserving and expanding freedom within a rule of law. They also reveal the essence of the man: strength as well as humility, firmness as well as compassion.

Some of these selections are famous and have become part of American iconography. His call for "the better angels" in the first inaugural, for a "new birth of freedom" in the Gettysburg Address, for "malice toward none; with charity for all" in the second inaugural are familiar. Some, like his notes on a law lecture and his letter to a little girl whose father died in combat, are less well known. Together they form a composite picture of Lincoln's thoughts and beliefs on crucial issues. Together, I hope, they form the essential Lincoln. Some incredibly wonderful pieces necessarily do not appear here—the wartime letters to his generals, for example. Though some selections appear here unabridged—his address at Cooper Union in February 1860, his August 1862 letter to Horace Greeley, the Gettysburg Address—many do not. The aim was not for completeness—that undertaking has been accomplished and all are urged to peruse it.* Rather, the selections chosen show the development of Lincoln's ideas, and consequently of Lincoln. Most are public speeches, some are letters intended to be read by the public, a few are private notes and correspondence. The Emancipation Proclamation was an executive order. Together they capture not only Lincoln's rightly renowned eloquence but also his ability to remain steadfastly true to certain fundamental principles even as, under the weight of politics, circumstances, and experience, he revised others. Some views remain constant but grow more clear and significant—his reliance on the Declaration of Independence, for instance. Others show change over time. While he never denied the inhumanity of slavery, his views about African Americans adjusted as he matured in office. Although he never claimed to know the will of God, he came to see himself as an instrument in God's plan.

Lincoln chose his words deliberately. Because Lincoln often addressed people who disagreed with him, he forced himself to clarify issues to their very core, their quintessential truth. He wrote to be understood; when his critics declared his rhetoric too simple, he told them that the people would understand. He wrote not to be popular but to persuade. Lincoln's faith in America's common folk, Northern laborer and Southern yeoman, was such that he was certain that if the implications of the possible choices facing the nation were made clear, they would do the right thing and democracy would thrive.

*Roy P. Basler, ed., *The Collected Works of Abraham Lincoln*, 8 vols. (New Brunswick: Rutgers University Press, 1953). The Abraham Lincoln Association published this set of Lincoln correspondence, and through its efforts the edition is now digital: www.papersofabrahamlincoln.org/reference.htm. The Lincoln Legal Papers are also available at the same website. There is also Mr. Lincoln's Virtual Library at the Library of Congress website: www.memory.loc.gov/ammem/alhtml/alrel.html. See also www.TheAgeofLincoln.com.

Lincoln relied on the Declaration of Independence for America's highest ideals. A corollary to the natural rights called for in the Declaration is Lincoln's belief in open opportunity for all—to benefit from their labor and to rise according to their work and ability. In precisely such an America Lincoln had risen from poverty, and he wanted to ensure that others had the same chance. Lincoln's commitment to freedom of opportunity protected under the law binds these writings together. Indeed, Lincoln's rational approach, derived from the rule of law and the Constitution, proved foundational to the preservation of the union. The rule of law represented a constant touchstone throughout Lincoln's life. It informed his understanding of liberty, which both deepened and broadened under the pressures of the Civil War. And it was Lincoln's understanding of liberty that became his greatest legacy of the age: The most enduring essence of Lincoln can be found in the constitutional amendments adopted after his assassination. Together, they enshrined the principle of personal liberty protected by the Constitution.

December 16, 2008

THE ESSENTIAL
LINCOLN

"To the People of Sangamo County"

March 9, 1832

The first known public writing of Abraham Lincoln captures the hardworking aspiring politician. He had lived in New Salem, Illinois (Sangamon County), only half a year and was not quite a month into his twenty-third year when he announced in the *Sangamo Journal* his campaign for a seat in the Illinois General Assembly. As a Whig he appeals to reason and addresses local issues—internal improvements, rising interest rates, and, notable for a man with less than a year's formal schooling, public education, declaring it "the most important subject which we as a people can be engaged in." He acknowledges having ambition, but, with a humility that would become a telling Lincolnian turn, he admits to his youth and inexperience and assures the public that if any of his ideas are wrong, he is willing to change his mind. Lincoln lost this first bid for the Illinois legislature but was elected two years later in 1834 with the second highest number of votes cast among thirteen candidates, and reelected in 1836, receiving the most votes of any candidate.

[ABRIDGED]

FELLOW CITIZENS: Having become a candidate for the honorable office of one of your representatives in the next General Assembly of this state, in accordance with an established custom and the principles of true republicanism, it becomes my duty to make known to you—the people whom I propose to represent—my sentiments with regard to local affairs.

Time and experience have verified to a demonstration, the public utility of internal improvements. That the poorest and most thinly populated countries would be greatly benefited by the opening of good roads and in the clearing of navigable streams within their limits is what no person will deny. But yet it is folly to undertake works of this or any other kind without first knowing that we are able to finish them—as half-finished work generally proves to be labor lost. There cannot justly be any objection to having railroads and canals, any more than to other good things, provided they cost nothing. The only objection is to paying for them, and the objection to paying arises from the want of ability to pay.

. . . Upon the subject of education, not presuming to dictate any plan or system respecting it, I can only say that I view it as the most important subject which we as a people can be engaged in. That every man may receive at least a moderate education and thereby be enabled to read the histories of his own and other countries, by which he may duly appreciate the value of our free institutions, appears to be an object of vital importance, even on this account alone, to say nothing of the advantages and satisfaction to be derived from all being able to read the Scriptures and other works, both of a religious and moral nature, for themselves. For my part, I desire to see the time when education and, by its means, morality, sobriety, enterprise, and industry shall become much more general than at present and should be gratified to have it in my power to contribute something to the advancement of any measure which might have a tendency to accelerate the happy period.

. . . But, Fellow Citizens, I shall conclude. Considering the great degree of modesty which should always attend youth, it is probable I have already been more presuming than becomes me. However, upon the subjects of which I have treated, I have spoken as I thought. I may be wrong in regard to any or all of them, but holding it a sound maxim that it is better to be only sometimes right than at all times wrong, so soon as I discover my opinions to be erroneous, I shall be ready to renounce them.

Every man is said to have his peculiar ambition. Whether it be true or not, I can say for one that I have no other so great as that of being truly esteemed of my fellow men, by rendering myself worthy of their esteem. How far I shall succeed in gratifying this ambition is yet to be developed. I am young and unknown to many of you. I was born and have ever remained in the most humble walks of life. I have no wealthy or popular relations to recommend me. My case is thrown exclusively upon the independent voters of this county, and if elected they will have conferred a favor upon me for which I shall be unremitting in my labors to compensate. But if the good people in their wisdom shall see fit to keep me in the background, I have been too familiar with disappointments to be very much chagrined. Your friend and fellow citizen,

A. LINCOLN.

Lyceum Speech at Springfield, Illinois

January 27, 1838

In September 1836, Lincoln received his license to practice law, and on April 15, 1837, he relocated to Springfield, Illinois, the new state capital, to join the law office of fellow Whig legislator John Todd Stuart. Nine months later, on January 27, 1838, he delivered his first public lecture, addressed to the Young Men's Lyceum. Displaying a loquaciousness he would subsequently prune, the young congressman stakes the nation's future on "a reverence for the Constitution and law" in contrast to the "mobocratic spirit" of the times. Evoking the specter of mass lynchings by unruly mobs, Lincoln calls on Americans to renew their patriotic attachment to sober reason, law and order, and the political edifice of liberty and equal rights bequeathed them by their forebearers. Here is boundless commitment to, if not necessarily blind faith in, general intelligence, sound morality, and reverence for the rule of law. And on its strengths, the twenty-eight-year-old Lincoln is prepared to assert that even "the gates of hell shall not prevail against it."

[ABRIDGED]

Address Before the Young Men's Lyceum of Springfield, Illinois
As a subject for the remarks of the evening, the perpetuation of our political institutions is selected.

In the great journal of things happening under the sun,

we, the American people, find our account running under the date of the nineteenth century of the Christian era. We find ourselves in the peaceful possession of the fairest portion of the earth as regards extent of territory, fertility of soil, and salubrity of climate. We find ourselves under the government of a system of political institutions conducing more essentially to the ends of civil and religious liberty than any of which the history of former times tells us. We, when mounting the stage of existence, found ourselves the legal inheritors of these fundamental blessings. We toiled not in the acquirement or establishment of them—they are a legacy bequeathed us by a once hardy, brave, and patriotic but now lamented and departed race of ancestors. Theirs was the task (and nobly they performed it) to possess themselves, and through themselves, us, of this goodly land, and to uprear upon its hills and its valleys a political edifice of liberty and equal rights; 'tis ours only to transmit these—the former, unprofaned by the foot of an invader, the latter undecayed by the lapse of time and untorn by usurpation—to the latest generation that fate shall permit the world to know. This task of gratitude to our fathers, justice to ourselves, duty to posterity, and love for our species in general all imperatively require us faithfully to perform.

How, then, shall we perform it? At what point shall we expect the approach of danger? By what means shall we fortify against it? Shall we expect some transatlantic military giant to step the ocean and crush us at a blow? Never! All the armies of Europe, Asia, and Africa combined, with all the treasure of the earth (our own excepted) in their military chest, with a Bonaparte for a commander, could not by force take a drink from the Ohio, or make a track on the Blue Ridge, in a trial of a thousand years.

At what point, then, is the approach of danger to be expected? I answer, if it ever reach us, it must spring up amongst us. It cannot come from abroad. If destruction be our lot, we must ourselves be its author and finisher. As a nation of freemen, we must live through all time, or die by suicide.

I hope I am overwary; but if I am not, there is, even now, something of ill omen amongst us. I mean the increasing disregard for law which pervades the country, the growing disposition to substitute the wild and furious passions in lieu of the sober judgment of courts, and the worse-than-savage mobs for the executive ministers of justice. This disposition is awfully fearful in any community, and that it now exists in ours, though grating to our feelings to admit, it would be a violation of truth and an insult to our intelligence to deny. Accounts of outrages committed by mobs form the everyday news of the times. They have pervaded the country, from New England to Louisiana—they are neither peculiar to the eternal snows of the former nor the burning suns of the latter—they are not the creature of climate—neither are they confined to the slaveholding or the nonslaveholding states. Alike, they spring up among the pleasure-hunting masters of Southern slaves and the order-loving citizens of the land of steady habits. Whatever, then, their cause may be, it is common to the whole country.

It would be tedious, as well as useless, to recount the horrors of all of them. Those happening in the state of Mississippi and at St. Louis are, perhaps, the most dangerous in example and revolting to humanity. In the Mississippi case, they first commenced by hanging the regular gamblers: a set of men certainly not following for a livelihood a very useful or very honest occupation, but one which, so far from being forbidden by the laws, was actually licensed by an act of the legislature passed but a single year before. Next, Negroes, suspected of conspiring to raise an insurrection, were caught up and hanged in all parts of the state; then, white men, supposed to be leagued with the Negroes; and finally, strangers from neighboring states going thither on business, were in many instances subjected to the same fate. Thus went on this process of hanging, from gamblers to Negroes, from Negroes to white citizens, and from these to strangers—till dead men were seen literally dangling from the boughs of trees upon every roadside and in numbers almost sufficient to rival the native Spanish moss of the country as a drapery of the forest.

Turn, then, to that horror-striking scene at St. Louis. A single victim was only sacrificed there. His story is very short and is, perhaps, the most highly tragic of anything of its length that has ever been witnessed in real life. A mulatto man, by the name of McIntosh, was seized in the street, dragged to the suburbs of the city, chained to a tree, and actually burned to death, and all within a single hour from the time he had been a freeman attending to his own business and at peace with the world.

Such are the effects of mob law, and such are the scenes becoming more and more frequent in this land so lately famed for love of law and order, and the stories of which have even now grown too familiar to attract anything more than an idle remark.

. . . Thus, then, by the operation of this mobocratic spirit, which all must admit is now abroad in the land, the strongest bulwark of any government, and particularly of those constituted like ours, may effectually be broken down and destroyed—I mean the attachment of the people. Whenever this effect shall be produced among us, whenever the vicious portion of population shall be permitted to gather in bands of hundreds and thousands and burn churches, ravage and rob provision stores, throw printing presses into rivers, shoot editors, and hang and burn obnoxious persons at pleasure, and with impunity, depend on it: This government cannot last. By such things, the feelings of the best citizens will become more or less alienated from it, and thus it will be left without friends, or with too few, and those few too weak to make their friendship effectual. At such a time and under such circumstances, men of sufficient tal[ent and ambition will not be want]ing to seize [the opportunity, strike the blow, and overturn that fair fabric] which for the last half century has been the fondest hope of the lovers of freedom throughout the world.

I know the American people are much attached to their government—I know they would suffer much for its sake—I know they would endure evils long and patiently before they would ever think of exchanging it for another. Yet, notwithstanding all this, if the laws be continually despised and disregarded, if their rights to be secure in their persons and property are held by no better tenure than the caprice of a mob, the alienation of their affections from the government is the natural consequence; and to that, sooner or later, it must come.

Here, then, is one point at which danger may be expected.

The question recurs, "How shall we fortify against it?" The answer is simple: Let every American, every lover of liberty, every well-wisher to his posterity swear by the blood of the revolution never to violate in the least particular the laws of the country, and never to tolerate their violation by others. As the patriots of seventy-six did to the support of the Declaration of Independence, so to the support of the Constitution and laws let every American pledge his life, his property, and his sacred honor—let every man remember that to violate the law is to trample on the blood of his father and to tear the character [charter?] of his own and his children's liberty—let reverence for the laws be breathed by every American mother to the lisping babe that prattles on her lap—let it be taught in schools, in seminaries, and in colleges—let it be written in primers, spelling books, and in almanacs—let it be preached from the pulpit, proclaimed in legislative halls, and enforced in courts of justice. And, in short, let it become the political religion of the nation, and let the old and the young, the rich and the poor, the grave and the gay, of all sexes and tongues and colors and conditions, sacrifice unceasingly upon its altars . . .

When I so pressingly urge a strict observance of all the laws, let me not be understood as saying there are no bad laws nor that grievances may not arise for the redress of which no legal provisions have been made. I mean to say no such thing. But I do mean to say that although bad laws, if they exist, should be repealed as soon as possible, still while they continue in force, for the sake of example, they should be religiously observed. So also in unprovided cases. If such arise, let proper legal provisions be made for them with the least possible delay, but, till then, let them if not too intolerable be borne with.

There is no grievance that is a fit object of redress by mob law. In any case that arises, as for instance, the promulgation of abolitionism, one of two positions is necessarily true; that is, the thing is right within itself and therefore deserves the protection of all law and all good citizens, or it is wrong and therefore proper to be prohibited by legal enactments; and in neither case is the interposition of mob law either necessary, justifiable, or excusable.

But, it may be asked, why suppose danger to our political institutions? Have we not preserved them for more than fifty years? And why may we not for fifty times as long?

We hope there is no sufficient reason. We hope all dangers may be overcome, but to conclude that no danger may ever arise would itself be extremely dangerous. There are now, and will hereafter be, many causes, dangerous in their tendency, which have not existed heretofore and which are not too insignificant to merit attention. That our government should have been maintained in its original form from its establishment until now is not much to be wondered at. It had many props to support it through that period, which now are decayed and crumbled away. Through that period, it was felt by all to be an undecided experiment; now, it is understood to be a successful one. Then, all that sought celebrity and fame and distinction expected to find them in the success of that experiment. Their all was staked upon it; their destiny was inseparably linked with it. Their ambition aspired to display before an admiring world a practical demonstration of the truth of a proposition which had hitherto been considered, at best, no better than problematical; namely, the capability of a people to govern themselves. If they succeeded, they were to be immortalized, their names were to be transferred to counties and cities and rivers and mountains, and to be revered and sung and toasted through all time. If they failed, they were to be called knaves and fools and fanatics for a fleeting hour, then to sink and be forgotten. They succeeded. The experiment is successful, and thousands have won their deathless names in making it so. But the game is caught, and I believe it is true that with the catching end the pleasures of the chase. This field of glory is harvested, and the crop is already appropriated. But new reapers will arise, and they too will seek a field. It is to deny what the history of the world tells us is true to suppose that men of ambition and talents will not continue to spring up amongst us. And, when they do, they will as naturally seek the gratification of their ruling passion as others have so done before them. The question then, is, can that gratification be found in supporting and maintaining an edifice that has been erected by others? Most certainly it cannot. Many great and good men sufficiently qualified for any task they should undertake may ever be found whose ambition would aspire to nothing beyond a seat in Congress, a gubernatorial or a presidential chair, but such belong not to the family of the lion or the tribe of the eagle. What! Think you these places would satisfy an Alexander, a Caesar, or a Napoleon? Never! Towering genius disdains a beaten path. It seeks regions hitherto unexplored. It sees no distinction in adding story to story upon the monuments of fame erected to the memory of others. It denies that it is glory enough to serve under any chief. It scorns to tread in the footsteps of any predecessor, however illustrious. It thirsts and burns for distinction, and, if possible, it will have it, whether at the expense of emancipating slaves or enslaving freemen. Is it unreasonable, then, to expect that some man possessed of the loftiest genius, coupled with ambition sufficient to push it to its utmost stretch, will at some time spring up among us? And when such a one does, it will require the people to be united with each other, attached to the government and laws, and generally intelligent to successfully frustrate his designs.

Distinction will be his paramount object, and although he would as willingly, perhaps more so, acquire it by doing good as harm, yet that opportunity being past and nothing left to be done in the way of building up, he would set boldly to the task of pulling down.

Here, then, is a probable case, highly dangerous and such a one as could not have well existed heretofore.

Another reason which once was, but which, to the same

extent, is now no more, has done much in maintaining our institutions thus far. I mean the powerful influence which the interesting scenes of the revolution had upon the passions of the people as distinguished from their judgment. By this influence, the jealousy, envy, and avarice incident to our nature and so common to a state of peace, prosperity, and conscious strength were, for the time, in a great measure smothered and rendered inactive, while the deep-rooted principles of hate and the powerful motive of revenge, instead of being turned against each other, were directed exclusively against the British nation. And thus, from the force of circumstances, the basest principles of our nature were either made to lie dormant or to become the active agents in the advancement of the noblest of cause[s?]—that of establishing and maintaining civil and religious liberty.

But this state of feeling must fade, is fading, has faded, with the circumstances that produced it.

I do not mean to say that the scenes of the revolution are now or ever will be entirely forgotten, but that like everything else they must fade upon the memory of the world and grow more and more dim by the lapse of time. In history, we hope, they will be read of and recounted so long as the Bible shall be read—but even granting that they will, their influence cannot be what it heretofore has been. Even then, they cannot be so universally known, nor so vividly felt, as they were by the generation just gone to rest. At the close of that struggle, nearly every adult male had been a participator in some of its scenes. The consequence was that of those scenes, in the form of a husband, a father, a son, or a brother, a living history was to be found in every family—a history bearing the indubitable testimonies of its own authenticity in the limbs mangled, in the scars of wounds received, in the midst of the very scenes related—a history too that could be read and understood alike by all, the wise and the ignorant, the learned and the unlearned. But those histories are gone. They can be read no more forever. They were a fortress of strength, but what invading foemen could never do, the silent artillery of time has done: the leveling of its walls. They are gone. They were a forest of giant oaks, but the all-resistless hurricane has swept over them and left only, here and there, a lonely trunk, despoiled of its verdure, shorn of its foliage, unshading and unshaded, to murmur in a few more gentle breezes and to combat with its mutilated limbs a few more ruder storms, then to sink and be no more.

. . . Passion has helped us but can do so no more. It will in future be our enemy. Reason, cold, calculating, unimpassioned reason, must furnish all the materials for our future support and defense. Let those [materials] be molded into general intelligence, [sound] morality and, in particular, a reverence for the Constitution and laws; and that we improved to the last, that we remained free to the last, that we revered his name to the last, [tha]t, during his long sleep, we permitted no hostile foot to pass over or desecrate [his] resting place shall be that which to le[arn the last] trump shall awaken our WASH[INGTON].

[Upon these] let the proud fabric of freedom r[est, as the] rock of its basis, and as truly as has been said of the only greater institution, "the gates of hell shall not prevail against it."

Handbill to the Voters of the Seventh Congressional District

July 31, 1846

Although his speeches and public writings include references to God, Lincoln was introspective about his faith. In his early years at New Salem, Lincoln read Thomas Paine's rationalist *The Age of Reason* and with the few local freethinkers debated the inerrancy of the Bible and Christ's divinity. Lincoln never joined a church, but this was not unusual at that time: Although 70 to 80 percent of Americans attended church or synagogue in 1860, only about half that number actually became members. Nevertheless, because of this, and because of his predilection for privacy, the press accused Lincoln of scoffing at Christianity when he ran for Congress in 1846 against a Methodist minister. To answer these rumors, Lincoln published a handbill, expounding his religious ideas, the only time he ever did so publicly.

[UNABRIDGED]

To the Voters of the Seventh Congressional District

FELLOW CITIZENS:

A charge having got into circulation in some of the neighborhoods of this district, in substance that I am an open scoffer at Christianity, I have by the advice of some friends concluded to notice the subject in this form. That I am not a member of any Christian church is true, but I have never denied the truth of the Scriptures, and I have never spoken with intentional disrespect of religion in general, or of any denomination of Christians in particular. It is true that in early life I was inclined to believe in what I understand is called the "doctrine of necessity"—that is, that the human mind is impelled to action, or held in rest, by some power over which the mind itself has no control—and I have sometimes (with one, two, or three but never publicly) tried to maintain this opinion in argument. The habit of arguing thus, however, I have entirely left off for more than five years. And I add here I have always understood this same opinion to be held by several of the Christian denominations. The foregoing is the whole truth, briefly stated, in relation to myself upon this subject.

I do not think I could myself be brought to support a man for office whom I knew to be an open enemy of, and scoffer at, religion. Leaving the higher matter of eternal consequences between him and his Maker, I still do not think any man has the right thus to insult the feelings and injure the morals of the community in which he may live. If, then, I was guilty of such conduct, I should blame no man who should condemn me for it, but I do blame those, whoever they may be, who falsely put such a charge in circulation against me.

A. LINCOLN.

Speech at Peoria, Illinois, on the Kansas-Nebraska Act

October 16, 1854

Lincoln retired from Congress in 1848 and concentrated on his legal practice, but passage of the Kansas-Nebraska Act in 1854 brought Lincoln back into the political fracas. This act meant the repeal of the Missouri Compromise of 1820, which, by determining where slavery could and could not exist in the Western territories, had muted sectional agitation for thirty-four years. The prime proponent of the new act, Senator Stephen A. Douglas of Illinois, instead introduced popular sovereignty as the means of determining slavery's expansion. He called it "the sacred right of self-government," although in his franker moments he said it was to make sure government was "for the benefit of white men and their posterity forever." In reply to Douglas, Abraham Lincoln said of popular sovereignty, "I hate it because of the monstrous injustice of slavery itself. I hate it because it deprives our republican example of its just influence in the world." In a lengthy speech that followed one by Douglas, Lincoln decries equating slaves with other property rights, asserting that slaves are humans, and that humans have the right of self-government. While most of Lincoln's arguments at Peoria would form the basis for his later speeches and writings, he will clearly change on one point. He states here, "Much as I hate slavery, I would consent to the extension of it rather than see the union dissolved . . ."

The repeal of the Missouri Compromise and the propriety of its restoration constitute the subject of what I am about to say.

As I desire to present my own connected view of this subject, my remarks will not be specifically an answer to Judge Douglas; yet, as I proceed, the main points he has presented will arise and will receive such respectful attention as I may be able to give them.

I wish further to say that I do not propose to question the patriotism or to assail the motives of any man or class of men, but rather to strictly confine myself to the naked merits of the question . . .

And, as this subject is no other than part and parcel of the larger general question of domestic slavery, I wish to MAKE and to KEEP the distinction between the EXISTING institution and the EXTENSION of it so broad and so clear that no honest man can misunderstand me, and no dishonest one successfully misrepresent me . . .

I think and shall try to show that it is wrong: wrong in its direct effect, letting slavery into Kansas and Nebraska, and wrong in its prospective principle, allowing it to spread to every other part of the wide world, where men can be found inclined to take it.

This *declared* indifference but, as I must think, covert *real* zeal for the spread of slavery I cannot but hate. I hate it because of the monstrous injustice of slavery itself. I hate it because it deprives our republican example of its just influence in the world—enables the enemies of free institutions, with plausibility, to taunt us as hypocrites—causes the real friends of freedom to doubt our sincerity—and especially because it forces so many really good men amongst ourselves into an open war with the very fundamental principles of civil liberty:

criticizing the Declaration of Independence and insisting that there is no right principle of action but *self-interest.*

Before proceeding, let me say I think I have no prejudice against the Southern people. They are just what we would be in their situation. If slavery did not now exist amongst them, they would not introduce it. If it did now exist amongst us, we should not instantly give it up. This I believe of the masses north and south. Doubtless there are individuals on both sides who would not hold slaves under any circumstances and others who would gladly introduce slavery anew if it were out of existence. We know that some Southern men do free their slaves, go north, and become tiptop abolitionists, while some Northern ones go south and become most cruel slave masters.

When Southern people tell us they are no more responsible for the origin of slavery than we, I acknowledge the fact. When it is said that the institution exists and that it is very difficult to get rid of it in any satisfactory way, I can understand and appreciate the saying. I surely will not blame them for not doing what I should not know how to do myself. If all earthly power were given me, I should not know what to do as to the existing institution. My first impulse would be to free all the slaves and send them to Liberia, to their own native land. But a moment's reflection would convince me that whatever of high hope (as I think there is) there may be in this, in the long run its sudden execution is impossible. If they were all landed there in a day, they would all perish in the next ten days, and there are not surplus shipping and surplus money enough in the world to carry them there in many times ten days. What then? Free them all and keep them among us as underlings? Is it quite certain that this betters their condition? I think I would not hold one in slavery, at any rate, yet the point is not clear enough for me to denounce people upon. What next?

Free them and make them politically and socially our equals? My own feelings will not admit of this, and if mine would, we well know that those of the great mass of white people will not. Whether this feeling accords with justice and sound judgment is not the sole question, if indeed it is any part of it. A universal feeling, whether well or ill founded, cannot be safely disregarded. We cannot, then, make them equals. It does seem to me that systems of gradual emancipation might be adopted, but for their tardiness in this I will not undertake to judge our brethren of the South.

When they remind us of their constitutional rights, I acknowledge them not grudgingly but fully and fairly, and I would give them any legislation for the reclaiming of their fugitives, which should not, in its stringency, be more likely to carry a freeman into slavery than our ordinary criminal laws are to hang an innocent one.

But all this, to my judgment, furnishes no more excuse for permitting slavery to go into our own free territory than it would for reviving the African slave trade by law. The law which forbids the bringing of slaves from Africa and that which has so long forbid the taking [of] them to Nebraska can hardly be distinguished on any moral principle, and the repeal of the former could find quite as plausible excuses as that of the latter . . .

I now come to consider whether the repeal, with its avowed principle, is intrinsically right. I insist that it is not . . . [In organizing Kansas and Nebraska] . . . it is proposed, and carried, to blot out the old dividing line of thirty-four years' standing and to open the whole of that country to the introduction of slavery. Now this, to my mind, is manifestly unjust. After an angry and dangerous controversy, the parties made friends by dividing the bone of contention. The one party first appropriates her own share, beyond all power to be disturbed in the possession of it, and then seizes the share of the other party. It is as if two starving men had divided their only loaf; the one had hastily swallowed his half and then grabbed the other half just as he was putting it to his mouth! . . .

Another LULLABY argument is that taking slaves to new countries does not increase their number, does not make anyone slave who otherwise would be free. There is some truth in this, and I am glad of it, but it [is] not WHOLLY true. The African slave trade is not yet effectually suppressed, and if we make a reasonable deduction for the white people amongst us who are foreigners and the descendants of foreigners arriving here since 1808, we shall find the increase of the black population outrunning that of the white to an extent unaccountable except by supposing that some of them too have been coming from Africa. If this be so, the opening of new countries to the institution increases the demand for and augments the price of slaves, and so does, in fact, make slaves of freemen by causing them to be brought from Africa and sold into bondage.

But, however this may be, we know the opening of new countries to slavery tends to the perpetuation of the institution and so does KEEP men in slavery who otherwise would be free. This result we do not FEEL like favoring, and we are under no legal obligation to suppress our feelings in this respect.

Equal justice to the South, it is said, requires us to consent to the extending of slavery to new countries. That is to say, inasmuch as you do not object to my taking my hog to Nebraska, therefore I must not object to you taking your slave. Now, I admit this is perfectly logical, if there is no difference between hogs and Negroes. But while you thus require me to deny the humanity of the Negro, I wish to ask whether you of the South yourselves have ever been willing to do as much? It is kindly provided that of all those who come into the world, only a small percentage are natural tyrants. That percentage is no larger in the slave states than in the free. The great majority, south as well as north, have human sympathies, of which they can no more divest themselves than they can of their sensibility to physical pain. These sympathies in the bosoms of the Southern people manifest in many ways their sense of the wrong of slavery and their consciousness that, after all, there is humanity in the Negro. If they deny this, let me address them a few plain questions. In 1820 you joined the North, almost unanimously, in declaring the African slave trade piracy and in annexing to it the punishment of death. Why did you do this? If you did not feel that it was wrong, why did you join in providing that men should be hung for it? The practice was no more than bringing wild Negroes from Africa to sell to such as would buy them. But you never thought of hanging men for catching and selling wild horses, wild buffaloes, or wild bears.

Again, you have amongst you a sneaking individual of the class of native tyrants known as the "SLAVE DEALER." He watches your necessities and crawls up to buy your slave at a speculating price. If you cannot help it, you sell to him; but if you can help it, you drive him from your door. You despise him utterly. You do not recognize him as a friend, or even as an honest man. Your children must not play with his; they may rollick freely with the little Negroes but not with the "slave dealer's" children. If you are obliged to deal with him, you try to get through the job without so much as touching him . . . Now why is this? You do not so treat the man who deals in corn, cattle, or tobacco . . .

And now, why will you ask us to deny the humanity of the slave? And estimate him only as the equal of the hog? Why ask us to do what you will not do yourselves? . . .

But one great argument in the support of the repeal of the Missouri Compromise is still to come. That argument is "the sacred right of self-government." It seems our distinguished senator has found great difficulty in getting his antagonists, even in the Senate, to meet him fairly on this argument—some poet has said, "Fools rush in where angels fear to tread."

At the hazard of being thought one of the fools of this quotation, I meet that argument—I rush in, I take that bull by the horns.

I trust I understand and truly estimate the right of self-government. My faith in the proposition that each man should do precisely as he pleases with all which is exclusively his own lies at the foundation of the sense of justice there is in me. I extend the principles to communities of men as well as to individuals. I so extend it because it is politically wise as well as naturally just; politically wise in saving us from broils about matters which do not concern us . . .

The doctrine of self-government is right—absolutely and eternally right—but it has no just application as here attempted. Or perhaps I should rather say that whether it has such just application depends upon whether a Negro is not or is a man. If he is not a man, why in that case he who is a man may, as a matter of self-government, do just as he pleases with him. But if the Negro is a man, is it not to that extent a total destruction of self-government to say that he too shall not govern himself? When the white man governs himself, that is self-government; but when he governs himself and also governs another man, that is more than self-government—that is despotism. If the Negro is a man, why then my ancient faith teaches me that "all men are created equal," and that there can be no moral right in connection with one man's making a slave of another.

Judge Douglas frequently, with bitter irony and sarcasm, paraphrases our argument by saying, "The white people of Nebraska are good enough to govern themselves, *but they are not good enough to govern a few miserable Negroes!*"

Well, I doubt not that the people of Nebraska are and will continue to be as good as the average of people elsewhere. I do not say to the contrary. What I do say is that no man is good enough to govern another man *without that other's consent.* I say this is the leading principle—the sheet anchor of American republicanism, our Declaration of Independence . . .

[A]ccording to our ancient faith the just powers of governments are derived from the consent of the governed. Now the relation of masters and slaves is, PRO TANTO, a total violation of this principle. The master not only governs the slave without his consent, but he governs him by a set of rules altogether different from those which he prescribes for himself. Allow ALL the governed an equal voice in the government, and that, and that only, is self-government.

Let it not be said I am contending for the establishment of political and social equality between the whites and blacks. I have already said the contrary. I am not now combating the argument of NECESSITY, arising from the fact that the blacks are already amongst us, but I am combating what is set up as MORAL argument for allowing them to be taken where they have never yet been—arguing against the EXTENSION of a bad thing, which where it already exists we must of necessity manage as we best can.

In support of his application of the doctrine of self-government, Senator Douglas has sought to bring to his aid the opinions and examples of our revolutionary fathers. I am glad he has done this. I love the sentiments of those old-time men and shall be most happy to abide by their opinions . . .

This same generation of men, and mostly the same individuals of the generation, who declared this principle—who declared independence—who fought the war of the revolution through—who afterward made the constitution under which we still live—these same men passed the ordinance of '87, declaring that slavery should never go to the Northwest Territory. I have no doubt Judge Douglas thinks they were very inconsistent in this. It is a question of discrimination between them and him. But there is not an inch of ground left for his claiming that their opinions—their example—their authority—are on his side in this controversy . . .

Another important objection to this application of the right of self-government is that it enables the first FEW to deprive the succeeding MANY of a free exercise of the right of self-government. The first few may get slavery IN, and the subsequent many cannot easily get it OUT. How common is the remark now in the slave states, "If we were only clear of our slaves, how much better it would be for us." They are actually deprived of the privilege of governing themselves as they would by the action of a very few in the beginning. The same thing was true of the whole nation at the time our Constitution was formed.

Whether slavery shall go into Nebraska or other new territories is not a matter of exclusive concern to the people who may go there. The whole nation is interested that the best use shall be made of these territories. We want them for the homes of free white people. This they cannot be, to any considerable extent, if slavery shall be planted within them. Slave states are places for poor white people to remove FROM, not to remove TO. New Free States are the places for poor people to go to and better their condition. For this use, the nation needs these territories.

Still further, there are constitutional relations between the slave and Free States, which are degrading to the latter. We are under legal obligations to catch and return their runaway slaves to them—a sort of dirty, disagreeable job which I believe, as a general rule, the slaveholders will not perform for one another. Then again, in the control of the government—the management of the partnership affairs—they have greatly the advantage of us. By the Constitution, each state has two senators, each has a number of representatives in proportion to the number of its people, and each has a number of presidential electors equal to the whole number of its senators and representatives together. But in ascertaining the number of the people for this purpose, five slaves are counted as being equal to three whites. The slaves do not vote; they are only counted and so used as to swell the influence of the white people's votes . . .

Now all this is manifestly unfair, yet I do not mention it to complain of it, insofar as it is already settled. It is in the Constitution, and I do not, for that cause or any other cause, propose to destroy, or alter, or disregard the Constitution. I stand to it, fairly, fully, and firmly . . .

Finally, I insist, that if there is ANYTHING which it is the duty of the WHOLE PEOPLE to never entrust to any hands but their own, that thing is the preservation and perpetuity of their own liberties and institutions. And if they shall think, as I do, that the extension of slavery endangers them more than any, or all, other causes, how recreant to themselves if they submit the question and, with it, the fate of their country to a mere handful of men bent only on temporary self-interest. If this question of slavery extension were an insignificant one—one having no power to do harm—it might be shuffled aside in this way. But being, as it is, the great behemoth of danger, shall the strong grip of the nation be loosened upon him to entrust him to the hands of such feeble keepers?

I have done with this mighty argument of self-government. Go, sacred thing! Go in peace.

But Nebraska is urged as a great union-saving measure. Well, I too go for saving the union. Much as I hate slavery, I would consent to the extension of it rather than see the union dissolved, just as I would consent to any GREAT evil to avoid a GREATER one. But when I go to union saving, I must believe at least that the means I employ has some adaptation to the end. To my mind, Nebraska has no such adaptation . . .

The Missouri Compromise ought to be restored. For the sake of the union, it ought to be restored. We ought to elect a House of Representatives which will vote its restoration. If by any means we omit to do this, what follows? Slavery may or may not be established in Nebraska. But whether it be or not, we shall have repudiated—discarded from the councils of the nation—the SPIRIT of COMPROMISE, for who after this will ever trust in a national compromise? The spirit of mutual concession—that spirit which first gave us the Constitution and which has thrice saved the union—we shall have strangled and cast from us forever. And what shall we have in lieu of it? The South flushed with triumph and tempted to excesses; the North betrayed, as they believe, brooding on wrong and burning for revenge. One side will provoke, the other resent. The one will taunt, the other defy; one aggresses, the other retaliates. Already a few in the North defy all constitutional restraints, resist the execution of the fugitive slave law, and even menace the institution of slavery in the states where it exists.

Already a few in the South claim the constitutional right to take to and hold slaves in the Free States, demand the revival of the slave trade, and demand a treaty with Great Britain by which fugitive slaves may be reclaimed from Canada. As yet they are but few on either side. It is a grave question for the lovers of the union whether the final destruction of the Missouri Compromise, and with it the spirit of all compromise, will or will not embolden and embitter each of these and fatally increase the numbers of both.

But restore the compromise, and what then? We thereby restore the national faith, the national confidence, the national feeling of brotherhood. We thereby reinstate the spirit of concession and compromise, that spirit which has never failed us in past perils and which may be safely trusted for all the future. The South ought to join in doing this. The peace of the nation is as dear to them as to us. In memories of the past and hopes of the future, they share as largely as we. It would be on their part, a great act—great in its spirit and great in its effect. It would be worth to the nation a hundred years' purchase of peace and prosperity . . .

Some men, mostly Whigs, who condemn the repeal of the Missouri Compromise nevertheless hesitate to go for its restoration lest they be thrown in company with the abolitionist. Will they allow me as an old Whig to tell them, good-humoredly, that I think this is very silly? Stand with anybody that stands RIGHT. Stand with him while he is right and PART with him when he goes wrong. Stand WITH the abolitionist in restoring the Missouri Compromise and stand AGAINST him when he attempts to repeal the fugitive slave law. In the latter case you stand with the Southern dis-unionist. What of that? You are still right. In both cases you are right. In both cases you oppose the dangerous extremes. In both you stand on middle ground and hold the ship level and steady . . .

Our republican robe is soiled, and trailed in the dust. Let us repurify it. Let us turn and wash it white in the spirit, if not the blood, of the revolution. Let us turn slavery from its claims of "moral right" back upon its existing legal rights and its arguments of "necessity." Let us return it to the position our fathers gave it and there let it rest in peace. Let us readopt the Declaration of Independence and with it the practices and policy which harmonize with it. Let North and South— let all Americans—let all lovers of liberty everywhere—join in the great and good work. If we do this, we shall not only have saved the union, but we shall have so saved it as to make and to keep it forever worthy of the saving. We shall have so saved it that the succeeding millions of free happy people the world over shall rise up and call us blessed to the latest generations.

5

Letter to Joshua Speed, Springfield, Illinois

August 24, 1855

In the summer of 1855, Lincoln wrote a candid and instructive letter to the man who was probably his closest friend, Kentuckian Joshua Speed. He juxtaposes his perspective on slavery with Speed's slaveowner's perspective. Lincoln ties his antislavery sentiments to the principles in the Declaration of Independence. He carries forward the extension of intolerance within a democracy to its logical, ugly conclusion. Although Lincoln disagrees strongly with his friend Speed, his letter's complimentary close is a reaffirmation of friendship.

[ABRIDGED]

Dear Speed:

You know what a poor correspondent I am. Ever since I received your very agreeable letter of the 22nd of May I have been intending to write you in answer to it. You suggest that in political action now, you and I would differ. I suppose we would; not quite as much, however, as you may think. You know I dislike slavery, and you fully admit the abstract wrong of it. So far there is no cause of difference. But you say that sooner than yield your legal right to the slave—especially at the bidding of those who are not themselves interested—you would see the union dissolved. I am not aware that *anyone* is bidding you to yield that right; very certainly *I* am not. I leave that matter entirely to yourself. I also acknowledge *your* rights and *my* obligations under the Constitution in regard to your slaves. I confess I hate to see the poor creatures hunted down, and caught, and carried back to their stripes and unrewarded toils, but I bite my lip and keep quiet. In 1841 you and I had together a tedious low-water trip on a steamboat from Louisville to St. Louis. You may remember, as I well do, that from Louisville to the mouth of the Ohio there were on board ten or a dozen slaves, shackled together with irons. That sight was a continual torment to me, and I see something like it every time I touch the Ohio or any other slave border. It is hardly fair for you to assume that I have no interest in a thing which has, and continually exercises, the power of making me miserable. You ought rather to appreciate how much the great body of the Northern people do crucify their feelings in order to maintain their loyalty to the Constitution and the union.

I do oppose the extension of slavery because my judgment and feelings so prompt me, and I am under no obligation to the contrary. If for this you and I must differ, differ we must. You say if you were president, you would send an army and hang the leaders of the Missouri outrages upon the Kansas elections; still, if Kansas fairly votes herself a slave state, she must be admitted, or the union must be dissolved. But how if she votes herself a slave state *unfairly*—that is, by the very means for which you say you would hang men? Must she still be admitted, or the union be dissolved? That will be the phase of the question when it first becomes a practical one. In your assumption that there may be a *fair* decision of the slavery question in Kansas, I plainly see you and I would differ about the Nebraska law. I look upon that enactment not as a *law* but as *violence* from the beginning. It was conceived in violence, passed in violence, is maintained in violence, and is being executed in violence. I say it was *conceived* in violence because the destruction of the Missouri Compromise, under the circumstances, was nothing less than violence. It was *passed* in violence because it could not have passed at all but for the votes of many members in violent disregard of the known will of their constituents. It is *maintained* in violence because the elections since clearly demand its repeal, and this demand is openly disregarded. *You* say men ought to be hung for the way they are executing that law, and *I* say the way it is being executed is quite as good as any of its antecedents. It is being executed in the precise way which was intended from the first; else why does no Nebraska man express astonishment or condemnation? . . .

That Kansas will form a slave constitution and, with it, will ask to be admitted into the union I take to be an already settled question, and so settled by the very means you so pointedly condemn. By every principle of law ever held by any court, North or South, every Negro taken to Kansas is free; yet in utter disregard of this—in the spirit of violence merely—that beautiful legislature gravely passes a law to hang men who shall venture to inform a Negro of his legal rights. This is the substance and real object of the law. If, like Haman, they should hang upon the gallows of their own building, I shall not be among the mourners for their fate.

In my humble sphere, I shall advocate the restoration of the Missouri Compromise so long as Kansas remains a territory; and when, by all these foul means, it seeks to come into the union as a slave state, I shall oppose it. I am very loath, in any case, to withhold my assent to the enjoyment of property *acquired* or *located* in good faith, but I do not admit that *good faith* in taking a Negro to Kansas to be held in slavery is a *pos-*

sibility with any man. Any man who has sense enough to be the controller of his own property has too much sense to misunderstand the outrageous character of this whole Nebraska business. But I digress. In my opposition to the admission of Kansas I shall have some company, but we may be beaten. If we are, I shall not, on that account, attempt to dissolve the union. On the contrary, if we succeed, there will be enough of us to take care of the union. I think it probable, however, we shall be beaten. Standing as a unit among yourselves, you can directly and indirectly bribe enough of our men to carry the day, as you could on an open proposition to establish monarchy. Get hold of some man in the North whose position and ability is such that he can make the support of your measure—whatever it may be—a *democratic party necessity*, and the thing is done . . .

You say if Kansas fairly votes herself a Free State, as a Christian you will rather rejoice at it. All decent slaveholders *talk* that way, and I do not doubt their candor. But they never *vote* that way. Although in a private letter or conversation you will express your preference that Kansas shall be free, you would vote for no man for Congress who would say the same thing publicly. No such man could be elected from any district in any slave state . . . The slave breeders and slave traders are a small, odious, and detested class among you, and yet in politics, they dictate the course of all of you and are as completely your masters as you are the masters of your own Negroes.

You inquire where I now stand. That is a disputed point. I think I am a Whig, but others say there are no Whigs and that I am an abolitionist. When I was at Washington I voted for the Wilmot Proviso as good as forty times, and I never heard of anyone attempting to un-Whig me for that. I now do no more than oppose the *extension* of slavery.

I am not a Know-Nothing. That is certain. How could I be? How can anyone who abhors the oppression of Negroes be in favor of degrading classes of white people? Our progress in degeneracy appears to me to be pretty rapid. As a nation, we began by declaring that *"all men are created equal."* We now practically read it "all men are created equal, *except Negroes.*" When the Know-Nothings get control, it will read "all men are created equal, except Negroes, *and foreigners, and Catholics.*" When it comes to this I should prefer emigrating to some country where they make no pretense of loving liberty—to Russia, for instance, where despotism can be taken pure and without the base alloy of hypocrisy.

Mary will probably pass a day or two in Louisville in October. My kindest regards to Mrs. Speed. On the leading subject of this letter, I have more of her sympathy than I have of yours.

And yet let [me] say I am Your friend forever

Λ. LINCOLN—

6

"Notes for a Law Lecture"

Undated fragment, probably 1859

The recipient of Lincoln's advice on how to be a good lawyer is unknown. It fits seamlessly, however, with the ethic Lincoln the politician would exemplify. Lincoln advocates diligence and hard work. When feasible, cases should be settled out of court by compromise. He recommends that lawyers promote peace and keep morality as a value and also offers advice on fees. His conclusion as to lawyers and honesty is classic Lincoln and one he would apply equally to politicians.

[UNABRIDGED]

I am not an accomplished lawyer. I find quite as much material for a lecture in those points wherein I have failed as in those wherein I have been moderately successful. The leading rule for the lawyer, as for the man of every other calling, is diligence. Leave nothing for tomorrow which can be done today. Never let your correspondence fall behind. Whatever piece of business you have in hand, before stopping do all the labor pertaining to it which can then be done. When you bring a common-law suit, if you have the facts for doing so, write the declaration at once. If a law point be involved, examine the books and note the authority you rely on upon the declaration itself, where you are sure to find it when wanted. The same of defenses and pleas. In business not likely to be litigated—ordinary collection cases, foreclosures, partitions, and the like—make all examinations of titles, and note them, and even draft orders and decrees in advance. This course has a triple advantage; it avoids omissions and neglect, saves your labor when once done, performs the labor out of court when you have leisure rather than in court when you have not. Extemporaneous speaking should be practiced and cultivated. It is the lawyer's avenue to the public. However able and faithful he may be in other respects, people are slow to bring him business if he cannot make a speech. And yet there is not a more fatal error to young lawyers than relying too much on speech making. If anyone, upon his rare powers of speaking, shall claim an exemption from the drudgery of the law, his case is a failure in advance.

Discourage litigation. Persuade your neighbors to compromise whenever you can. Point out to them how the nominal winner is often a real loser—in fees, expenses, and waste of time. As a peacemaker, the lawyer has a superior opportunity of being a good man. There will still be business enough.

Never stir up litigation. A worse man can scarcely be found than one who does this. Who can be more nearly a fiend than he who habitually overhauls the register of deeds in search of defects in titles, whereon to stir up strife and put money in his pocket? A moral tone ought to be infused into the profession, which should drive such men out of it.

The matter of fees is important, far beyond the mere question of bread and butter involved. Properly attended to, fuller justice is done to both lawyer and client. An exorbitant fee should never be claimed. As a general rule never take your whole fee in advance nor any more than a small retainer. When fully paid beforehand, you are more than a common mortal if you can feel the same interest in the case as if something was still in prospect for you, as well as for your client. And when you lack interest in the case the job will very likely lack skill and diligence in the performance. Settle the amount of fee and take a note in advance. Then you will feel that you are working for something, and you are sure to do your work faithfully and well. Never sell a fee note, at least not before the consideration service is performed. It leads to negligence and dishonesty—negligence by losing interest in the case and dishonesty in refusing to refund when you have allowed the consideration to fail.

There is a vague popular belief that lawyers are necessarily dishonest. I say vague, because when we consider to what extent confidence and honors are reposed in and conferred upon lawyers by the people, it appears improbable that their impression of dishonesty is very distinct and vivid. Yet the impression is common, almost universal. Let no young man choosing the law for a calling for a moment yield to the popular belief. Resolve to be honest at all events, and if in your own judgment you cannot be an honest lawyer, resolve to be honest without being a lawyer. Choose some other occupation rather than one in the choosing of which you do, in advance, consent to be a knave.

7

"A House Divided" Speech at Springfield, Illinois

June 16, 1858

The Bible recounts the trouble Jesus got into when, in the midst of doing good works and casting out demons, he declared, "A house divided against itself cannot stand." In citing these words Lincoln knew that he was throwing down the gauntlet. Advisers strongly urged him to edit that statement out of his speech: It was too radical and too provocative, a seeming advocation of sectional war. Lincoln was insistent that it remain. The idea that the United States could not remain half free, half slave distressed and angered many, who pointed out that it had been doing just that quite nicely for eighty-two years. Lincoln spoke, however, at a unique time in American history. The Kansas-Nebraska Act's repeal of the Missouri Compromise and the Supreme Court's decision in the Dred Scott case, declaring that all blacks—slave and free—could never be United States citizens and that slavery could not be prohibited from the Western territories, seemed fundamentally to alter the legal and moral landscape.

[ABRIDGED]

Mr. PRESIDENT and Gentlemen of the Convention.

If we could first know where we are and whither we are tending, we could then better judge what to do and how to do it.

We are now far into the fifth year since a policy was initiated with the avowed object and confident promise of putting an end to slavery agitation.

Under the operation of that policy, that agitation has not only not ceased but has constantly augmented.

In my opinion, it will not cease until a crisis shall have been reached and passed.

"A house divided against itself cannot stand."

I believe this government cannot endure, permanently half slave and half free.

I do not expect the union to be dissolved—I do not expect the house to fall—but I do expect it will cease to be divided.

It will become all one thing or all the other.

Either the opponents of slavery will arrest the further spread of it and place it where the public mind shall rest in the belief that it is in course of ultimate extinction, or its advocates will push it forward till it shall become alike lawful in all the states, old as well as new, North as well as South.

Have we no tendency to the latter condition?

Let anyone who doubts carefully contemplate that now almost complete legal combination—piece of machinery, so to speak—compounded of the Nebraska doctrine and the Dred Scott decision. Let him consider not only what work the machinery is adapted to do and how well adapted, but also let him study the history of its construction and trace, if he can, or rather fail, if he can, to trace the evidences of design and concert of action among its chief bosses from the beginning . . .

The working points of that machinery are:

First, that no Negro slave, imported as such from Africa, and no descendant of such slave can ever be a citizen of any state, in the sense of that term as used in the Constitution of the United States.

This point is made in order to deprive the Negro, in every

possible event, of the benefit of this provision of the United States Constitution, which declares that—

"The citizens of each state shall be entitled to all privileges and immunities of citizens in the several states."

Secondly, that "subject to the Constitution of the United States," neither Congress nor a territorial legislature can exclude slavery from any United States territory.

This point is made in order that individual men may fill up the territories with slaves without danger of losing them as property, and thus to enhance the chances of permanency to the institution through all the future.

Thirdly, that whether the holding a Negro in actual slavery in a Free State makes him free, as against the holder, the United States courts will not decide but will leave to be decided by the courts of any slave state the Negro may be forced into by the master.

This point is made not to be pressed immediately. But if acquiesced in for a while, and apparently endorsed by the people at an election, then to sustain the logical conclusion that what Dred Scott's master might lawfully do with Dred Scott, in the Free State of Illinois, every other master may lawfully do with any other one or one thousand slaves in Illinois or in any other Free State.

Auxiliary to all this, and working hand in hand with it, the Nebraska doctrine, or what is left of it, is to educate and mold public opinion, at least Northern public opinion, to not care whether slavery is voted down or voted up.

This shows exactly where we now are, and partially also whither we are tending . . .

We cannot absolutely know that all these exact adaptations are the result of preconcert. But when we see a lot of framed timbers, different portions of which we know have been gotten out at different times and places and by differ-ent workmen—Stephen, Franklin, Roger, and James,* for in-stance—and when we see these timbers joined together, and see they exactly make the frame of a house or a mill, all the tenons and mortises exactly fitting and all the lengths and proportions of the different pieces exactly adapted to their re-spective places, and not a piece too many or too few—not omitting even scaffolding—or, if a single piece be lacking, we can see the place in the frame exactly fitted and prepared to yet bring such piece in—in such a case, we find it impossible to not believe that Stephen and Franklin and Roger and James all understood one another from the beginning and all worked upon a common plan or draft drawn up before the first lick was struck . . .

In what cases the power of the states is so restrained by the U.S. Constitution is left an open question, precisely as the same question as to the restraint on the power of the territo-ries was left open in the Nebraska act. Put that and that to-gether, and we have another nice little niche, which we may ere long see filled with another Supreme Court decision, de-claring that the Constitution of the United States does not permit a state to exclude slavery from its limits.

And this may especially be expected if the doctrine of "care not whether slavery be voted down or voted up" shall gain upon the public mind sufficiently to give promise that such a decision can be maintained when made.

Such a decision is all that slavery now lacks of being alike lawful in all the states.

Welcome or unwelcome, such decision is probably com-

*Stephen A. Douglas, Franklin Pierce, Roger Taney, and James Buchanan.

ing and will soon be upon us, unless the power of the present political dynasty shall be met and overthrown.

We shall lie down pleasantly dreaming that the people of Missouri are on the verge of making their state free, and we shall awake to the reality, instead, that the Supreme Court has made Illinois a slave state.

To meet and overthrow the power of that dynasty is the work now before all those who would prevent that consummation.

That is what we have to do.

But how can we best do it? . . .

Two years ago the Republicans of the nation mustered over thirteen hundred thousand strong.

We did this under the single impulse of resistance to a common danger, with every external circumstance against us.

Of strange, discordant, and even hostile elements, we gathered from the four winds and formed and fought the battle through, under the constant hot fire of a disciplined, proud, and pampered enemy.

Did we brave all then to falter now? Now, when that same enemy is wavering, dissevered, and belligerent?

The result is not doubtful. We shall not fail—if we stand firm, we shall not fail . . .

8

Speech at Chicago, Illinois

July 10, 1858

Once Douglas learned that Lincoln would be his opponent for the Senate in 1858, he turned his considerable talents toward discrediting him, beginning his attack on July 9, 1858, in Chicago. Citing Lincoln's "House Divided" speech, Douglas accused Lincoln of advocating civil war.

The following evening, from the same Chicago balcony, Lincoln responded. After clarifying his house divided statement, he becomes more animated in refuting Douglas's assertion that the U.S. government was "made by the white man, for the benefit of the white man, to be administered by white men." Lincoln the politician arguably overplays his hand; throwing caution to the wind, he claims remarkable privilege for the Declaration of Independence and its implications about race and equality. Douglas promptly turned this back on Lincoln, indignantly proclaiming, "This Chicago doctrine of Lincoln's—declaring that the Negro and the white man are made equal by the Declaration of Independence and by Divine Providence—is a monstrous heresy."

[ABRIDGED]

... We are now a mighty nation. We are thirty—or about thirty—millions of people, and we own and inhabit about one-fifteenth part of the dry land of the whole earth. We run our memory back over the pages of history for about eighty-two years and we discover that we were then a very small people in point of numbers, vastly inferior to what we are now, with a vastly less extent of country, with vastly less of everything we deem desirable among men. We look upon the change as exceedingly advantageous to us and to our posterity, and we fix upon something that happened away back as in some way or other being connected with this rise of prosperity. We find a race of men living in that day whom we claim as our fathers and grandfathers. They were iron men; they fought for the principle that they were contending for, and we understood that by what they then did it has followed that the degree of prosperity that we now enjoy has come to us. We hold this annual celebration to remind ourselves of all the good done in this process of time, of how it was done and who did it, and how we are historically connected with it, and we go from these meetings in better humor with ourselves— we feel more attached the one to the other and more firmly bound to the country we inhabit. In every way we are better men in the age and race and country in which we live for these celebrations. But after we have done all this we have not yet reached the whole. There is something else connected with it. We have besides these men—descended by blood from our ancestors—among us perhaps half our people who are not descendants at all of these men; they are men who have come from Europe—German, Irish, French, and Scandinavian—men that have come from Europe themselves or whose ancestors have come hither and settled here, finding themselves our equals in all things. If they look back through this history to trace their connection with those days by blood, they find they have none; they cannot carry themselves back into that glorious epoch and make themselves feel that they are part of us. But when they look through that old

Declaration of Independence they find that those old men say that, "We hold these truths to be self-evident, that all men are created equal," and then they feel that that moral sentiment taught in that day evidences their relation to those men, that it is the father of all moral principle in them, and that they have a right to claim it as though they were blood of the blood and flesh of the flesh of the men who wrote that Declaration [loud and long continued applause], and so they are. That is the electric cord in that Declaration that links the hearts of patriotic and liberty-loving men together, that will link those patriotic hearts as long as the love of freedom exists in the minds of men throughout the world.

Now, sirs, for the purpose of squaring things with this idea of "don't care if slavery is voted up or voted down," for sustaining the Dred Scott decision, for holding that the Declaration of Independence did not mean anything at all, we have Judge Douglas giving his exposition of what the Declaration of Independence means, and we have him saying that the people of America are equal to the people of England. According to his construction, you Germans are not connected with it. Now I ask you in all soberness, if all these things, if indulged in, if ratified, if confirmed and endorsed, if taught to our children and repeated to them, do not tend to rub out the sentiment of liberty in the country and to transform this government into a government of some other form. Those arguments that are made, that the inferior race are to be treated with as much allowance as they are capable of enjoying, that as much is to be done for them as their condition will allow— what are these arguments? They are the arguments that kings have made for enslaving the people in all ages of the world. You will find that all the arguments in favor of king craft were of this class; they always bestrode the necks of the people, not that they wanted to do it, but because the people were better off for being ridden. That is their argument, and this argument of the judge is the same old serpent that says you work and I eat, you toil and I will enjoy the fruits of it. Turn in whatever way you will—whether it come from the mouth of a king, an excuse for enslaving the people of his country, or from the mouth of men of one race as a reason for enslaving the men of another race—it is all the same old serpent, and I hold if that course of argumentation that is made for the purpose of convincing the public mind that we should not care about this should be granted, it does not stop with the Negro. I should like to know if taking this old Declaration of Independence which declares that all men are equal upon principle, and making exceptions to it, where will it stop. If one man says it does not mean a Negro, why not another say it does not mean some other man? If that Declaration is not the truth, let us get the statute book in which we find it and tear it out! Who is so bold as to do it! If it is not true, let us tear it out! Let us stick to it then. Let us stand firmly by it then.

It may be argued that there are certain conditions that make necessities and impose them upon us, and to the extent that a necessity is imposed upon a man he must submit to it. I think that was the condition in which we found ourselves when we established this government. We had slavery among us, we could not get our Constitution unless we permitted them to remain in slavery, we could not secure the good we did secure if we grasped for more, and having by necessity submitted to that much, it does not destroy the principle that is the charter of our liberties. Let that charter stand as our standard.

My friend has said to me that I am a poor hand to quote Scripture. I will try it again, however. It is said in one of the admonitions of the Lord, "As your Father in Heaven is perfect, be ye also perfect." The Savior, I suppose, did not expect that any human creature could be perfect as the Father in Heaven, but He said, "As your Father in Heaven is perfect, be ye also perfect." He set that up as a standard, and he who did most toward reaching that standard attained the highest degree of moral perfection. So I say in relation to the principle that all men are created equal, let it be as nearly reached as we can. If we cannot give freedom to every creature, let us do nothing that will impose slavery upon any other creature. Let us then turn this government back into the channel in which the framers of the Constitution originally placed it. Let us stand firmly by each other. If we do so we are turning in the contrary direction that our friend Judge Douglas proposes—not intentionally—as working in the traces tend to make this one universal slave nation. He is one that runs in that direction, and as such I resist him.

My friends, I have detained you about as long as I desired to do, and I have only to say, let us discard all this quibbling about this man and the other man—this race and that race and the other race being inferior, and therefore they must be placed in an inferior position—discarding our standard that we have left us. Let us discard all these things and unite as one people throughout this land until we shall once more stand up declaring that all men are created equal.

My friends, I could not, without launching off upon some new topic, which would detain you too long, continue to-night. I thank you for this most extensive audience that you have furnished me tonight. I leave you, hoping that the lamp of liberty will burn in your bosoms until there shall no longer be a doubt that all men are created free and equal.

9

Lincoln-Douglas Debates

Autumn 1858

The Lincoln-Douglas debates presented two visions of democracy. Stephen A. Douglas and the Democrats offered pure white supremacy, Abraham Lincoln a more inclusive vision of liberty and democracy.

In each of the seven formal debates, one speaker led off for an hour, the other spoke for an hour and a half, and then the first speaker had the last thirty minutes. The state of Illinois included northern territory friendly to Lincoln and southern territory friendly to Douglas. It was the more neutral ground in central Illinois that both candidates needed for electoral victory.

Douglas denounced Lincoln's extraordinary suggestion in his Chicago speech on July 10 to "discard all this quibbling" about race and to declare "that all men are created equal." Douglas found a ready audience; in 1848, more than two-thirds of Illinois voters had approved a constitutional amendment to exclude even free African Americans from the state. The old Whig territory in the middle of the state was very much opposed to abolition, and both Douglas and Lincoln understood that no man who declared equality for blacks could be elected to a statewide office. Republicans advised Lincoln to back away from his call for equality, and Lincoln did.

In this fourth debate at Charleston, Lincoln made statements that still haunt today. In his meanest pronouncement on race, he denied that he favored civil rights for African Americans. Yet he kept his ground in declaring that the Declaration of Independence included all men in its claim for natural rights. Douglas's plan of attack was to make certain that voters understood that those natural rights inevitably led to civil rights. In the last three debates, Lincoln went on the offense and became bolder on African American rights. In Alton, Lincoln eloquently cast slavery as a moral issue.

Fourth joint debate, Charleston, September 18, 1858. Lincoln went first, and his words were reported in the Press & Tribune.

[ABRIDGED]

While I was at the hotel today, an elderly gentleman called upon me to know whether I was really in favor of producing a perfect equality between the Negroes and white people. While I had not proposed to myself on this occasion to say much on that subject, yet as the question was asked me I thought I would occupy perhaps five minutes in saying something in regard to it. I will say then that I am not, nor ever have been, in favor of bringing about in any way the social and political equality of the white and black races, that I am not nor ever have been in favor of making voters or jurors of Negroes, nor of qualifying them to hold office, nor to intermarry with white people; and I will say in addition to this that there is a physical difference between the white and black races which I believe will forever forbid the two races living together on terms of social and political equality. And inasmuch as they cannot so live, while they do remain together there must be the position of superior and inferior, and I as much as any other man am in favor of having the superior position assigned to the white race. I say upon this occasion I do not perceive that because the white man is to have the superior position the Negro should be denied everything. I do not understand that because I do not want a Negro woman for a slave I must necessarily want her for a wife. My understanding is that I can just let her alone. I am now in my fiftieth year, and I certainly never have had a black woman for either a slave or a wife. So it seems to me quite possible for us to get along without making either slaves or wives of Negroes. I will add to this that I have never seen to my knowledge a man, woman, or child who was in favor of producing a perfect equality, social and political, between Negroes and white men. I recollect of but one distinguished instance that I ever heard of so frequently as to be entirely satisfied of its correctness, and that is the case of Judge Douglas's old friend Col. Richard M. Johnson. I will also add to the remarks I have made (for I am not going to enter at large upon this subject) that I have never had the least apprehension that I or my friends would marry Negroes if there was no law to keep them from it, but as Judge Douglas and his friends seem to be in great apprehension that they might if there were no law to keep them from it, I give him the most solemn pledge that I will to the very last stand by the law of this state which forbids the marrying of white people with Negroes. I will add one further word, which is this, that I do not understand there is any place where an alteration of the social and political relations of the Negro and the white man can be made except in the state legislature— not in the Congress of the United States—and as I do not really apprehend the approach of any such thing myself, and as Judge Douglas seems to be in constant horror that some such danger is rapidly approaching, I propose as the best means to prevent it that the judge be kept at home and placed in the state legislature to fight the measure. I do not propose dwelling longer at this time on this subject . . .

Fellow Citizens—It follows as a matter of course that a half-hour answer to a speech of an hour and a half can be but a very hurried one. I shall only be able to touch upon a few of the points suggested by Judge Douglas and give them a brief attention, while I shall have to totally omit others for the want of time.

Judge Douglas has said to you that he has not been able to get from me an answer to the question whether I am in favor of Negro citizenship. So far as I know, the judge never asked me the question before. He shall have no occasion to ever ask it again, for I tell him very frankly that I am not in favor of Negro citizenship. This furnishes me an occasion for saying a few words upon the subject. I mentioned in a certain speech of mine, which has been printed, that the Supreme Court had decided that a Negro could not possibly be made a citizen, and without saying what was my ground of complaint in regard to that, or whether I had any ground of complaint, Judge Douglas has from that thing manufactured nearly everything that he ever says about my disposition to produce an equality between the Negroes and the white people. If anyone will read my speech, he will find I mentioned that as one of the points decided in the course of the Supreme Court opinions, but I did not state what objection I had to it. But Judge Douglas tells the people what my objection was when I did not tell them myself. Now, my opinion is that the different states have the power to make a Negro a citizen under the Constitution of the United States if they choose. The Dred Scott decision decides that they have not that power. If the state of Illinois had that power, I should be opposed to the exercise of it. That is all I have to say about it.

Judge Douglas has told me that he heard my speeches north and my speeches south—that he had heard me at Ottawa and at Freeport in the North and recently at Jonesboro in the South, and there was a very different cast of sentiment in the speeches made at the different points. I will not charge upon Judge Douglas that he willfully misrepresents me, but I call upon every fair-minded man to take these speeches and read them, and I dare him to point out any difference between my printed speeches north and south. While I am here perhaps I ought to say a word, if I have the time, in regard to the latter portion of the judge's speech, which was a sort of declamation in reference to my having said I entertained the belief that this government would not endure half slave and half free. I have said so and I did not say it without what seemed to me to be good reasons. It perhaps would require more time than I have now to set forth these reasons in detail, but let me ask you a few questions. Have we ever had any peace on this slavery question? When are we to have peace upon it if it is kept in the position it now occupies? How are we ever to have peace upon it? That is an important question. To be sure, if we will all stop and allow Judge Douglas and his friends to march on in their present career until they plant the institution all over the nation, here and wherever else our flag waves, and we acquiesce in it, there will be peace. But let me ask Judge Douglas how he is going to get the people to do that? They have been wrangling over this question for at least forty years. This was the cause of the agitation resulting in the Missouri Compromise; this produced the troubles at the annexation of Texas, in the acquisition of the territory acquired in the Mexican war. Again, this was the trouble which was quieted by the Compromise of 1850, when it was settled "forever," as both the great political parties declared in their national conventions. That "forever" turned out to be just four years, when Judge Douglas himself reopened it. When is it likely to come to an end? He introduced the Nebraska bill in 1854 to put another end to the slavery agitation. He promised that it would finish it all up immediately, and he has never made a speech since until he got into a quarrel with the president about the Lecompton Constitution, in which he has not declared that we are just at the end of the slavery agitation. But in one speech, I think last winter, he did say that he didn't quite see when the end of the slavery agitation would come. Now he tells us again that it is all over, and the people of Kansas have voted down the Lecompton Constitution. How is it over? That was only one of the attempts at putting an end to the slavery agitation, one of these "final settlements." Is Kansas in the union? Has she formed a constitution that she is likely to come in under? Is not the slavery agitation still an open question in that territory? Has the voting down of that constitution put an end to all the trouble? Is that more likely to settle it than every one of these previous attempts to settle the slavery agitation? Now, at this day in the history of the world we can no more foretell where the end of this slavery agitation will be than we can see the end of the world itself. The Nebraska-Kansas bill was introduced four years and a half ago, and if the agitation is ever to come to an end, we may say we are four years and a half nearer the end. So too we can say we are four years and a half nearer the end of the world, and we can just as clearly see the end of the world as we can see the end of this agitation. The Kansas settlement did not conclude it. If Kansas should sink today and leave a great vacant space in the earth's surface, this vexed question would still be among us. I say, then, there is no way of putting an end to the slavery agitation amongst us but to put it back upon the basis where our fathers placed it, no way but to keep it out of our new territories—to restrict it forever to the old states where it now exists. Then the public mind will rest in the belief that it is in the course of ultimate extinction. That is one way of putting an end to the slavery agitation.

The other way is for us to surrender and let Judge Douglas and his friends have their way and plant slavery over all the states, cease speaking of it as in any way a wrong, regard slavery as one of the common matters of property, and speak of Negroes as we do of our horses and cattle. But while it drives on in its state of progress as it is now driving, and as it has driven for the last five years, I have ventured the opinion, and I say today, that we will have no end to the slavery agitation until it takes one turn or the other. I do not mean that when it takes a turn toward ultimate extinction it will be in a day, nor in a year, nor in two years. I do not suppose that in the most peaceful way ultimate extinction would occur in less than a hundred years at the least, but that it will occur in the best way for both races in God's own good time, I have no doubt. But, my friends, I have used up more of my time than I intended on this point.

Seventh, and last joint debate, Alton, October 15, 1858. Douglas was the first speaker, and then Lincoln replied, his words reported in the Press & Tribune.

[ABRIDGED]

You have heard him frequently allude to my controversy with him in regard to the Declaration of Independence. I confess that I have had a struggle with Judge Douglas on that matter, and I will try briefly to place myself right in regard to it on this occasion . . .

I think the authors of that notable instrument intended to include all men, but they did not mean to declare all men equal in all respects. They did not mean to say all men were equal in color, size, intellect, moral development, or social capacity. They defined with tolerable distinctness in what they did consider all men created equal—equal in certain inalienable rights, among which are life, liberty, and the pursuit of happiness. This they said, and this they meant. They did not mean to assert the obvious untruth, that all were then actually enjoying that equality, nor yet that they were about to confer it immediately upon them. In fact they had no power to confer such a boon. They meant simply to declare the right so that the enforcement of it might follow as fast as circumstances should permit . . .

Again, the institution of slavery is only mentioned in the Constitution of the United States two or three times, and in neither of these cases does the word "slavery" or "Negro race" occur; but covert language is used each time, and for a purpose full of significance. What is the language in regard to the prohibition of the African slave trade? It runs in about this way: "The migration or importation of such persons as any of the states now existing shall think proper to admit, shall not be prohibited by the Congress prior to the year one thousand eight hundred and eight."

The next allusion in the Constitution to the question of slavery and the black race is on the subject of the basis of representation, and there the language used is, "Representatives and direct taxes shall be apportioned among the several states which may be included within this union, according to their respective numbers, which shall be determined by adding to the whole number of free persons, including those bound to service for a term of years, and excluding Indians not taxed— three-fifths of all other persons."

It says "persons," not slaves, not Negroes, but this "three-fifths" can be applied to no other class among us than the Negroes.

Lastly, in the provision for the reclamation of fugitive slaves it is said, "No person held to service or labor in one state under the laws thereof escaping into another shall in consequence of any law or regulation therein be discharged from such service or labor, but shall be delivered up on claim of the party to whom such service or labor may be due." There again, there is no mention of the word "Negro" or of slavery. In all three of these places, being the only allusions to slavery in the instrument, covert language is used. Language is used not suggesting that slavery existed or that the black race were among us. And I understand the contemporaneous history of those times to be that covert language was used with a purpose, and that purpose was that in our Constitution, which it was hoped and is still hoped will endure forever—when it should be read by intelligent and patriotic men after the institution of slavery had passed from among us— there should be nothing on the face of the great charter of liberty suggesting that such a thing as Negro slavery had ever existed among us. This is part of the evidence that the fathers of the government expected and intended the institution of slavery to come to an end. They expected and intended that it should be in the course of ultimate extinction. And when I say that I desire to see the further spread of it arrested, I only say I desire to see that done which the fathers have first done. When I say I desire to see it placed where the public mind will rest in the belief that it is in the course of ultimate extinction, I only say I desire to see it placed where they placed it. It is not true that our fathers, as Judge Douglas assumes, made this government part slave and part free. Understand the sense in which he puts it. He assumes that slavery is a rightful thing within itself, was introduced by the framers of the Constitution. The exact truth is that they found the institution existing among us, and they left it as they found it. But in making the government, they left this institution with many clear marks of disapprobation upon it. They found slavery among them and they left it among them because of the difficulty—the absolute impossibility—of its immediate removal. And when Judge Douglas asks me why we cannot let it remain part slave and part free as the fathers of the government made, he asks a question based upon an assumption which is itself a falsehood. And I turn upon him and ask him the question, when the policy that the fathers of the government had adopted in relation to this element among us was the best policy in the world—the only wise policy, the only policy that we can ever safely continue upon that will ever give us peace unless this dangerous element masters us all and becomes a national institution—I turn upon him and ask him why he could not let it alone? I turn and ask him why he was driven to the necessity of introducing a new policy in regard to it? . . . I ask him why he could not let it remain where our fathers placed it? I ask too of Judge Douglas and his friends why we shall not again place this institution upon the basis on which the fathers left it? I ask you when he infers that I am in favor of setting the Free and slave states at war, when the institution was placed in that attitude by those who made the Constitution, did they make any war? If we had no war out of it when thus placed, wherein is the ground of belief that we shall have war out of it if we return to that policy? Have we had any peace upon this matter springing from any other basis? I maintain that we have not. I have proposed nothing more than a return to the policy of the fathers.

I confess, when I propose a certain measure of policy, it is not enough for me that I do not intend anything evil in the result, but it is incumbent on me to show that it has not a tendency to that result. I have met Judge Douglas in that point of view. I have not only made the declaration that I do not mean to produce a conflict between the states, but I have tried to show by fair reasoning, and I think I have shown to the minds of fair men, that I propose nothing but what has a most peaceful tendency. The quotation that I happened to make in that Springfield speech, that "a house divided against itself cannot stand," and which has proved so offensive to the judge, was part and parcel of the same thing. He tries to show that variety in the domestic institutions of the different states is necessary and indispensable. I do not dispute it. I have no controversy with Judge Douglas about that. I shall very readily agree with him that it would be foolish for us to insist upon having a cranberry law here in Illinois, where we have no cranberries, because they have a cranberry law in Indiana, where they have cranberries. I should insist that it would be exceedingly wrong in us to deny to Virginia the right to enact oyster laws where they have oyster, because we want no such laws here. I understand, I hope, quite as well as Judge Douglas or anybody else that the variety in the soil and climate and face of the country, and consequent variety in the industrial pursuits and productions of a country, require systems of law conforming to this variety in the natural features of the country. I understand quite as well as Judge Douglas that if we here raise a barrel of flour more than we want, and the Louisianans raise a barrel of sugar more than they want, it is of mutual advantage to exchange. That produces commerce, brings us together, and makes us better friends. We like one another the more for it. And I understand as well as Judge Douglas, or anybody else, that these mutual accommodations are the cements which bind together the different parts of this union, that instead of being a thing to "divide the house"— figuratively expressing the union—they tend to sustain it; they are the props of the house tending always to hold it up . . .

Now, irrespective of the moral aspect of this question as to whether there is a right or wrong in enslaving a Negro, I am still in favor of our new territories being in such a condition that white men may find a home—may find some spot where they can better their condition—where they can settle upon new soil and better their condition in life. I am in favor of this not merely (I must say it here as I have elsewhere) for our own people who are born amongst us, but as an outlet for free white people everywhere, the world over, in which Hans and Baptiste and Patrick, and all other men from all the world, may find new homes and better their conditions in life . . .

On this subject of treating it as a wrong, and limiting its spread, let me say a word. Has anything ever threatened the existence of this union save and except this very institution of slavery? What is it that we hold most dear amongst us? Our own liberty and prosperity. What has ever threatened our liberty and prosperity save and except this institution of slavery? If this is true, how do you propose to improve the condition of things by enlarging slavery, by spreading it out and making it bigger? You may have a wen or a cancer upon your person and not be able to cut it out lest you bleed to death, but surely it is no way to cure it, to engraft it and spread it over your whole body. That is no proper way of treating what you regard a wrong . . .

They are the two principles that have stood face-to-face from the beginning of time and will ever continue to struggle. The one is the common right of humanity and the other the divine right of kings. It is the same principle in whatever shape it develops itself. It is the same spirit that says, "You work and toil and earn bread, and I'll eat it." No matter in what shape it comes, whether from the mouth of a king who seeks to bestride the people of his own nation and live by the fruit of their labor or from one race of men as an apology for enslaving another race, it is the same tyrannical principle. I was glad to express my gratitude at Quincy, and I reexpress it here to Judge Douglas, that he looks to no end of the institution of slavery. That will help the people to see where the struggle really is. It will hereafter place with us all men who really do wish the wrong may have an end. And whenever we can get rid of the fog which obscures the real question— when we can get Judge Douglas and his friends to avow a policy looking to its perpetuation—we can get out from among them that class of men and bring them to the side of those who treat it as a wrong. Then there will soon be an end of it, and that end will be its "ultimate extinction."

10

Letter to Henry L. Pierce and Others

April 6, 1859

Unable to attend the Jefferson Day dinner at Boston, Lincoln mailed this letter to be read at the gathering. Lincoln distinguishes between the rights of people and of property and argues that while Republicans support both, his party privileges man over money, a theme he will continue to develop in his later writing. Given his turn for storytelling and humorous anecdotes, Lincoln includes in this political commentary an amusing story to position the Republican Party as the true heir of Jefferson. This letter illustrates Lincoln's reverence for the Declaration of Independence. As he phrases it, "All honor to Jefferson," who introduced "an abstract truth, applicable to all men and all times." The Declaration of Independence would be the touchstone of Lincoln's philosophy, and his greatest legacy would be the placement of the Declaration of Independence into the Constitution, the ideal of personal liberty now a guarantee.

[UNABRIDGED]

Messrs. Henry L. Pierce, & others. Springfield, Ills.

Gentlemen

Your kind note inviting me to attend a festival in Boston, on the 13th inst. in honor of the birthday of Thomas Jefferson, was duly received. My engagements are such that I cannot attend.

Bearing in mind that about seventy years ago, two great political parties were first formed in this country, that Thomas Jefferson was the head of one of them, and Boston the headquarters of the other, it is both curious and interesting that those supposed to descend politically from the party opposed to Jefferson should now be celebrating his birthday in their own original seat of empire, while those claiming political descent from him have nearly ceased to breathe his name everywhere.

Remembering too that the Jefferson party were formed upon their supposed superior devotion to the personal rights of men, holding the rights of property to be secondary only and greatly inferior, and then assuming that the so-called Democracy of today are the Jefferson, and their opponents the anti-Jefferson parties, it will be equally interesting to note how completely the two have changed hands as to the principle upon which they were originally supposed to be divided.

The Democracy of today hold the liberty of one man to be absolutely nothing when in conflict with another man's right of property. Republicans, on the contrary, are for both the man and the dollar, but in cases of conflict, the man before the dollar.

I remember once being much amused at seeing two partially intoxicated men engage in a fight with their greatcoats on, which fight, after a long and rather harmless contest, ended in each having fought himself out of his own coat and into that of the other. If the two leading parties of this day are really identical with the two in the days of Jefferson and Adams, they have performed about the same feat as the two drunken men.

But soberly, it is now no child's play to save the principles of Jefferson from total overthrow in this nation.

One would start with great confidence that he could convince any sane child that the simpler propositions of Euclid are true, but, nevertheless, he would fail utterly with one who should deny the definitions and axioms. The principles of Jefferson are the definitions and axioms of free society. And yet they are denied and evaded, with no small show of success. One dashingly calls them "glittering generalities," another bluntly calls them "self-evident lies," and still others insidiously argue that they apply only to "superior races."

These expressions, differing in form, are identical in object and effect—the supplanting the principles of free government and restoring those of classification, caste, and legitimacy. They would delight a convocation of crowned heads plotting against the people. They are the vanguard—the miners and sappers—of returning despotism. We must repulse them, or they will subjugate us.

This is a world of compensations, and he who would be no slave must consent to have no slave. Those who deny freedom to others deserve it not for themselves and, under a just God, cannot long retain it.

All honor to Jefferson—to the man who, in the concrete pressure of a struggle for national independence by a single people, had the coolness, forecast, and capacity to introduce into a merely revolutionary document an abstract truth applicable to all men and all times, and so to embalm it there, that today, and in all coming days, it shall be a rebuke and a stumbling block to the very harbingers of reappearing tyranny and oppression.

Your obedient Servant A. LINCOLN—

11

Address to the Wisconsin State Agricultural Society

September 30, 1859

Though as a young man Lincoln escaped farmwork as quickly as possible, when invited to speak at the Wisconsin Agricultural Society, he declared his respect for "the great calling of agriculture." In a long address during which Lincoln waxes philosophical on steam power and (again) the importance of education, foreshadowing land-grant colleges, he also offers up his views on capital and labor. Lincoln here answers an address by the prominent Southern planter Senator James Henry Hammond of South Carolina, who in 1858 declared that every society required a laboring or "mudsill class" so that others could enjoy the fruits of higher civilization. This mudsill theory runs counter to Lincoln's view of free labor, wherein each person has an equal opportunity to benefit from his own work. Lincoln recommends agricultural cultivation, as well as intellectual and moral cultivation, as a way to secure prosperity and happiness. Lincoln's approach combines practicality with a faith in mankind's innate goodness.

[ABRIDGED]

. . . I presume I am not expected to employ the time assigned me in the mere flattery of the farmers as a class. My opinion of them is that, in proportion to numbers, they are neither better nor worse than other people. In the nature of things they are more numerous than any other class, and I believe there really are more attempts at flattering them than any other; the reason of which I cannot perceive, unless it be that they can cast more votes than any other. On reflection, I am not quite sure that there is not cause of suspicion against you in selecting me, in some sort a politician and in no sort a farmer, to address you.

But farmers being the most numerous class, it follows that their interest is the largest interest. It also follows that that interest is most worthy of all to be cherished and cultivated— that if there be inevitable conflict between that interest and any other, that other should yield . . .

The world is agreed that labor is the source from which human wants are mainly supplied. There is no dispute upon this point. From this point, however, men immediately diverge. Much disputation is maintained as to the best way of applying and controlling the labor element. By some it is assumed that labor is available only in connection with capital—that nobody labors unless somebody else, owning capital, somehow by the use of that capital induces him to do it. Having assumed this, they proceed to consider whether it is best that capital shall hire laborers and thus induce them to work by their own consent, or buy them and drive them to it without their consent. Having proceeded so far they naturally conclude that all laborers are necessarily either hired laborers or slaves. They further assume that whoever is once a hired laborer is fatally fixed in that condition for life, and thence again that his condition is as bad as or worse than that of a slave. This is the "mudsill" theory.

But another class of reasoners hold the opinion that there is no such relation between capital and labor as assumed, and that there is no such thing as a freeman being fatally fixed for life in the condition of a hired laborer, that both these as-sumptions are false and all inferences from them groundless. They hold that labor is prior to, and independent of, capital; that, in fact, capital is the fruit of labor and could never have existed if labor had not first existed—that labor can exist with-out capital, but that capital could never have existed without labor. Hence they hold that labor is the superior—greatly the superior—of capital.

They do not deny that there is, and probably always will be, a relation between labor and capital. The error, as they hold, is in assuming that the whole labor of the world exists within that relation: A few men own capital, and that few avoid labor themselves, and with their capital hire, or buy, an-other few to labor for them. A large majority belong to neither class—neither work for others nor have others working for them. Even in all our slave states, except South Carolina, a majority of the whole people of all colors are neither slaves nor masters. In these Free States, a large majority are nei-ther hirers nor hired. Men, with their families—wives, sons, and daughters—work for themselves on their farms, in their houses, and in their shops, taking the whole product to them-selves and asking no favors of capital on the one hand nor of hirelings or slaves on the other. It is not forgotten that a con-siderable number of persons mingle their own labor with cap-ital, that is, labor with their own hands and also buy slaves or hire freemen to labor for them, but this is only a mixed and not a distinct class. No principle stated is disturbed by the existence of this mixed class. Again, as has already been said, the opponents of the "mudsill" theory insist that there is not, of necessity, any such thing as the free hired laborer being fixed to that condition for life. There is demonstration for say-ing this. Many independent men in this assembly doubtless a few years ago were hired laborers. And their case is almost if not quite the general rule.

The prudent, penniless beginner in the world labors for wages awhile, saves a surplus with which to buy tools or land for himself, then labors on his own account another while, and at length hires another new beginner to help him. This, say its advocates, is free labor—the just and generous and prosperous system which opens the way for all, gives hope to all, and energy, and progress, and improvement of condition to all. If any continue through life in the condition of the hired laborer, it is not the fault of the system but because of either a dependent nature which prefers it or improvidence, folly, or singular misfortune. I have said this much about the elements of labor generally as introductory to the consideration of a new phase which that element is in process of assuming. The old general rule was that educated people did not perform manual labor. They managed to eat their bread, leaving the toil of producing it to the uneducated. This was not an insupportable evil to the working bees, so long as the class of drones remained very small. But now, especially in these Free States, nearly all are educated—quite too nearly all to leave the labor of the uneducated in any [way] adequate to the support of the whole. It follows from this that henceforth educated people must labor. Otherwise, education itself would become a positive and intolerable evil. No country can sustain in idleness more than a small percentage of its numbers. The great majority must labor at something productive. From these premises the problem springs, "How can labor and education be the most satisfactorily combined?"

By the "mudsill" theory it is assumed that labor and education are incompatible, and any practical combination of them impossible. According to that theory, a blind horse upon a treadmill is a perfect illustration of what a laborer should be—all the better for being blind, that he could not tread out of place or kick understandingly. According to that theory, the education of laborers is not only useless but pernicious and dangerous. In fact, it is, in some sort, deemed a misfortune that laborers should have heads at all. Those same heads are regarded as explosive materials only to be safely kept in damp places as far as possible from that peculiar sort of fire which ignites them. A Yankee who could invent a strong-handed man without a head would receive the everlasting gratitude of the "mudsill" advocates.

But free labor says "no!" Free labor argues that, as the Author of man makes every individual with one head and one pair of hands, it was probably intended that heads and hands should cooperate as friends, and that that particular head should direct and control that particular pair of hands. As each man has one mouth to be fed, and one pair of hands to furnish food, it was probably intended that that particular pair of hands should feed that particular mouth—that each head is the natural guardian, director, and protector of the hands and mouth inseparably connected with it, and that being so, every head should be cultivated and improved by whatever will add to its capacity for performing its charge. In one word free labor insists on universal education.

I have so far stated the opposite theories of "mudsill" and "free labor" without declaring any preference of my own between them. On an occasion like this I ought not to declare any. I suppose, however, I shall not be mistaken in assuming as a fact that the people of Wisconsin prefer free labor, with its natural companion, education.

This leads to the further reflection that no other human occupation opens so wide a field for the profitable and agreeable combination of labor with cultivated thought as agriculture. I know of nothing so pleasant to the mind as the discovery of anything which is at once new and valuable—nothing which so lightens and sweetens toil as the hopeful pursuit of such discovery. And how vast and how varied a field is agriculture for such discovery. The mind, already trained to thought in the country school or higher school, cannot fail to find there an exhaustless source of profitable enjoyment. Every blade of grass is a study, and to produce two where there was but one is both a profit and a pleasure. And not grass alone, but soils, seeds, and seasons—hedges, ditches, and fences, draining, droughts, and irrigation—plowing, hoeing, and harrowing—reaping, mowing, and threshing—saving crops, pests of crops, diseases of crops, and what will prevent or cure them—implements, utensils, and machines, their relative merits, and [how] to improve them—hogs, horses, and cattle—sheep, goats, and poultry—trees, shrubs, fruits, plants, and flowers—the thousand things of which these are specimens, each a world of study within itself.

In all this, book learning is available. A capacity and taste for reading gives access to whatever has already been discovered by others. It is the key, or one of the keys, to the already solved problems.

And not only so. It gives a relish and facility for successfully pursuing the unsolved ones. The rudiments of science are available and highly valuable. Some knowledge of botany assists in dealing with the vegetable world, with all growing crops. Chemistry assists in the analysis of soils, selection, and application of manures, and in numerous other ways. The mechanical branches of natural philosophy are ready help in almost everything, but especially in reference to implements and machinery.

The thought recurs that education—cultivated thought—can best be combined with agricultural labor, or any labor, on the principle of thorough work—that careless, half-performed, slovenly work makes no place for such combination. And thorough work, again, renders sufficient the smallest quantity of ground to each man. And this again conforms to what must occur in a world less inclined to wars and more devoted to the arts of peace than heretofore. Population must increase rapidly—more rapidly than in former times—and ere long the most valuable of all arts will be the art of deriving a comfortable subsistence from the smallest area of soil. No community whose every member possesses this art can ever be the victim of oppression in any of its forms. Such community will be alike independent of crowned kings, money kings, and land kings.

But according to your program, the awarding of premiums awaits the closing of this address. Considering the deep interest necessarily pertaining to that performance, it would be no wonder if I am already heard with some impatience. I will detain you but a moment longer. Some of you will be successful, and such will need but little philosophy to take them home in cheerful spirits; others will be disappointed and will be in a less happy mood. To such, let it be said, "Lay it not too much to heart." Let them adopt the maxim, "Better luck next time," and then, by renewed exertion, make that better luck for themselves.

And by the successful, and the unsuccessful, let it be remembered that while occasions like the present bring their sober and durable benefits, the exultations and mortifications of them are but temporary; that the victor shall soon be the vanquished if he relax in his exertion; and that the vanquished this year may be victor the next, in spite of all competition.

It is said an Eastern monarch once charged his wise men to invent him a sentence, to be ever in view, and which should be true and appropriate in all times and situations. They presented him the words: "And this, too, shall pass away." How much it expresses! How chastening in the hour of pride! How consoling in the depths of affliction! "And this, too, shall pass away." And yet let us hope it is not quite true. Let us hope, rather, that by the best cultivation of the physical world beneath and around us, and the intellectual and moral world within us, we shall secure an individual, social, and political prosperity and happiness whose course shall be onward and upward and which, while the earth endures, shall not pass away.

12

Speech at Cooper Union, New York City

February 27, 1860

Delivering a speech to a crowd in New York was the opportunity for Lincoln to prove his mettle to a wide audience of political leaders and sophisticated Easterners. He prepared carefully and even purchased a new black suit. Lincoln, who cared deeply about shaping public opinion, uses clear and compelling arguments and avoids the radical metaphors of his "House Divided" speech. Instead, his analysis of slavery and the Founding Fathers moves along conservative lines. The speech struck a resounding cord. Although much of the speech is directed "to the Southern people," Lincoln was also addressing the same call for reasonableness to his Northern listeners. Few knew prior to this speech that Lincoln had presidential aspirations, but with its delivery he advanced substantially closer to that goal.

[UNABRIDGED]

Address at Cooper Institute, New York City

MR. PRESIDENT AND FELLOW CITIZENS OF NEW YORK: The facts with which I shall deal this evening are mainly old and familiar, nor is there anything new in the general use I shall make of them. If there shall be any novelty, it will be in the mode of presenting the facts and the inferences and observations following that presentation.

In his speech last autumn, at Columbus, Ohio, as reported in *The New York Times*, Senator Douglas said:

"Our fathers, when they framed the government under which we live, understood this question just as well and even better than we do now."

I fully endorse this, and I adopt it as a text for this discourse. I so adopt it because it furnishes a precise and an agreed starting point for a discussion between Republicans and that wing of the Democracy headed by Senator Douglas. It simply leaves the inquiry: "What was the understanding those fathers had of the question mentioned?"

What is the frame of government under which we live?

The answer must be: "The Constitution of the United States." That Constitution consists of the original, framed in 1787 (and under which the present government first went into operation), and twelve subsequently framed amendments, the first ten of which were framed in 1789.

Who were our fathers that framed the Constitution? I suppose the "thirty-nine" who signed the original instrument may be fairly called our fathers who framed that part of the present government. It is almost exactly true to say they framed it, and it is altogether true to say they fairly represented the opinion and sentiment of the whole nation at that time. Their names, being familiar to nearly all and accessible to quite all, need not now be repeated.

I take these "thirty-nine" for the present, as being "our fathers who framed the government under which we live."

What is the question which, according to the text, those fathers understood "just as well and even better than we do now"?

It is this: Does the proper division of local from federal authority, or anything in the Constitution, forbid our federal government to control as to slavery in our federal territories?

Upon this, Senator Douglas holds the affirmative and Republicans the negative. This affirmation and denial form an issue, and this issue—this question—is precisely what the text declares our fathers understood "better than we."

Let us now inquire whether the "thirty-nine," or any of them, ever acted upon this question, and if they did, how they acted upon it, how they expressed that better understanding?

In 1784, three years before the Constitution—the United States then owning the Northwestern Territory and no other—the Congress of the Confederation had before them the question of prohibiting slavery in that territory, and four of the "thirty-nine" who afterward framed the Constitution were in that Congress and voted on that question. Of these, Roger Sherman, Thomas Mifflin, and Hugh Williamson voted for the prohibition, thus showing that, in their understanding, no line dividing local from federal authority, nor anything else, properly forbade the federal government to control as to slavery in federal territory. The other of the four—James M'Henry—voted against the prohibition, showing that for some cause he thought it improper to vote for it.

In 1787, still before the Constitution, but while the Convention was in session framing it, and while the Northwestern Territory still was the only territory owned by the United States, the same question of prohibiting slavery in the territory again came before the Congress of the Confederation, and two more of the "thirty-nine" who afterward signed the Constitution were in that Congress and voted on the question. They were William Blount and William Few, and they both voted for the prohibition—thus showing that, in their understanding, no line dividing local from federal authority, nor anything else, properly forbade the federal government to control as to slavery in federal territory. This time the prohibition became a law, being part of what is now well known as the Ordinance of '87.

The question of federal control of slavery in the territories seems not to have been directly before the Convention which framed the original Constitution, and hence it is not recorded that the "thirty-nine," or any of them, while engaged on that instrument expressed any opinion of that precise question.

In 1789, by the first Congress which sat under the Constitution, an act was passed to enforce the Ordinance of '87, including the prohibition of slavery in the Northwestern Territory. The bill for this act was reported by one of the "thirty-nine," Thomas Fitzsimmons, then a member of the House of Representatives from Pennsylvania. It went through all its stages without a word of opposition and finally passed both branches without yeas and nays, which is equivalent to an unanimous passage. In this Congress there were sixteen of the thirty-nine fathers who framed the original Constitution. They were John Langdon, Nicholas Gilman, Wm. S. Johnson, Roger Sherman, Robert Morris, Thos. Fitzsimmons, William Few, Abraham Baldwin, Rufus King, William Paterson, George Clymer, Richard Bassett, George Read, Pierce Butler, Daniel Carroll, James Madison.

This shows that, in their understanding, no line dividing local from federal authority, nor anything in the Constitution, properly forbade Congress to prohibit slavery in the federal territory; else both their fidelity to correct principle, and their oath to support the Constitution, would have constrained them to oppose the prohibition.

Again, George Washington, another of the "thirty-nine," was then president of the United States and, as such, approved and signed the bill, thus completing its validity as a law and thus showing that, in his understanding, no line dividing local from federal authority, nor anything in the Constitution, forbade the federal government to control as to slavery in federal territory.

No great while after the adoption of the original Constitution, North Carolina ceded to the federal government the country now constituting the state of Tennessee; and a few years later Georgia ceded that which now constitutes the states of Mississippi and Alabama. In both deeds of cession it was made a condition by the ceding states that the federal government should not prohibit slavery in the ceded country. Besides this, slavery was then actually in the ceded country. Under these circumstances, Congress, on taking charge of these countries, did not absolutely prohibit slavery within them. But they did interfere with it—take control of it—even there, to a certain extent. In 1798, Congress organized the territory of Mississippi. In the act of organization, they prohibited the bringing of slaves into the territory from anyplace without the United States by fine and giving freedom to slaves so brought. This act passed both branches of Congress without yeas and nays. In that Congress were three of the "thirty-nine" who framed the original Constitution. They were John Langdon, George Read, and Abraham Baldwin. They all, probably, voted for it. Certainly they would have placed their opposition to it upon record if, in their understanding, any line dividing local from federal authority, or anything in the Constitution, properly forbade the federal government to control as to slavery in federal territory.

In 1803, the federal government purchased the Louisiana country. Our former territorial acquisitions came from certain of our own states, but this Louisiana country was acquired from a foreign nation. In 1804, Congress gave a territorial organization to that part of it which now constitutes the state of

Louisiana. New Orleans, lying within that part, was an old and comparatively large city. There were other considerable towns and settlements, and slavery was extensively and thoroughly intermingled with the people. Congress did not, in the Territorial Act, prohibit slavery, but they did interfere with it—take control of it—in a more marked and extensive way than they did in the case of Mississippi. The substance of the provision therein made in relation to slaves was:

First. That no slave should be imported into the territory from foreign parts. Second. That no slave should be carried into it who had been imported into the United States since the first day of May 1798. Third. That no slave should be carried into it except by the owner and for his own use as a settler; the penalty in all the cases being a fine upon the violator of the law and freedom to the slave.

This act also was passed without yeas and nays. In the Congress which passed it, there were two of the "thirty-nine." They were Abraham Baldwin and Jonathan Dayton. As stated in the case of Mississippi, it is probable they both voted for it. They would not have allowed it to pass without recording their opposition to it if, in their understanding, it violated either the line properly dividing local from federal authority, or any provision of the Constitution.

In 1819–20 came and passed the Missouri question. Many votes were taken, by yeas and nays, in both branches of Congress upon the various phases of the general question. Two of the "thirty-nine"—Rufus King and Charles Pinckney—were members of that Congress. Mr. King steadily voted for slavery prohibition and against all compromises, while Mr. Pinckney as steadily voted against slavery prohibition and against all compromises. By this, Mr. King showed that, in his understanding, no line dividing local from federal authority, nor anything in the Constitution, was violated by Congress prohibiting slavery in federal territory; while Mr. Pinckney, by his votes, showed that, in his understanding, there was some sufficient reason for opposing such prohibition in that case.

The cases I have mentioned are the only acts of the "thirty-nine," or of any of them, upon the direct issue which I have been able to discover.

To enumerate the persons who thus acted—as being four in 1784, two in 1787, seventeen in 1789, three in 1798, two in 1804, and two in 1819–20—there would be thirty of them. But this would be counting John Langdon, Roger Sherman, William Few, Rufus King, and George Read each twice, and Abraham Baldwin three times. The true number of those of the "thirty-nine" whom I have shown to have acted upon the question, which, by the text, they understood better than we, is twenty-three, leaving sixteen not shown to have acted upon it in any way.

Here, then, we have twenty-three out of our thirty-nine fathers "who framed the government under which we live," who have, upon their official responsibility and their corporal oaths, acted upon the very question which the text affirms they "understood just as well and even better than we do now," and twenty-one of them—a clear majority of the whole "thirty-nine"—so acting upon it as to make them guilty of gross political impropriety and willful perjury if, in their understanding, any proper division between local and federal authority, or anything in the Constitution they had made themselves and sworn to support, forbade the federal government to control as to slavery in the federal territories. Thus the twenty-one acted. And as actions speak louder than words, so actions, under such responsibility, speak still louder.

Two of the twenty-three voted against congressional prohibition of slavery in the federal territories, in the instances in which they acted upon the question. But for what reasons they so voted is not known. They may have done so because they thought a proper division of local from federal authority, or some provision or principle of the Constitution, stood in the way; or they may, without any such question, have voted against the prohibition on what appeared to them to be sufficient grounds of expediency. No one who has sworn to support the Constitution can conscientiously vote for what he understands to be an unconstitutional measure, however expedient he may think it. But one may and ought to vote against a measure which he deems constitutional if, at the same time, he deems it inexpedient. It therefore would be unsafe to set down even the two who voted against the prohibition as having done so because, in their understanding, any proper division of local from federal authority, or anything in the Constitution, forbade the federal government to control as to slavery in federal territory.

The remaining sixteen of the "thirty-nine," so far as I have discovered, have left no record of their understanding upon the direct question of federal control of slavery in the federal territories. But there is much reason to believe that their understanding upon that question would not have appeared different from that of their twenty-three compeers had it been manifested at all.

For the purpose of adhering rigidly to the text, I have purposely omitted whatever understanding may have been manifested by any person, however distinguished, other than the thirty-nine fathers who framed the original Constitution, and, for the same reason, I have also omitted whatever understanding may have been manifested by any of the "thirty-nine" even on any other phase of the general question of slavery. If we should look into their acts and declarations on those other phases, as the foreign slave trade and the morality and policy of slavery generally, it would appear to us that on the direct question of federal control of slavery in federal territories, the sixteen, if they had acted at all, would probably have acted just as the twenty-three did. Among that sixteen were several of the most noted antislavery men of those times—as Dr. Franklin, Alexander Hamilton, and Gouverneur Morris—while there was not one now known to have been otherwise, unless it may be John Rutledge of South Carolina.

The sum of the whole is that of our thirty-nine fathers who framed the original Constitution, twenty-one—a clear majority of the whole—certainly understood that no proper division of local from federal authority, nor any part of the Constitution, forbade the federal government to control slavery in the federal territories, while all the rest probably had the same understanding. Such, unquestionably, was the understanding of our fathers who framed the original Constitution, and the text affirms that they understood the question "better than we."

But so far I have been considering the understanding of the question manifested by the framers of the original Constitution. In and by the original instrument, a mode was provided for amending it, and, as I have already stated, the present frame of "the government under which we live" consists of that original and twelve amendatory articles framed and adopted since. Those who now insist that federal control of slavery in federal territories violates the Constitution point us to the provisions which they suppose it thus violates, and, as I understand, they all fix upon provisions in these amendatory articles and not in the original instrument. The Supreme Court in the Dred Scott case plant themselves upon the Fifth

Amendment, which provides that no person shall be deprived of "life, liberty or property without due process of law," while Senator Douglas and his peculiar adherents plant themselves upon the Tenth Amendment, providing that "the powers not delegated to the United States by the Constitution," "are reserved to the states respectively, or to the people."

Now, it so happens that these amendments were framed by the first Congress which sat under the Constitution, the identical Congress which passed the act already mentioned enforcing the prohibition of slavery in the Northwestern Territory. Not only was it the same Congress, but they were the identical, same individual men who, at the same session and at the same time within the session, had under consideration and in progress toward maturity these constitutional amendments and this act prohibiting slavery in all the territory the nation then owned. The constitutional amendments were introduced before and passed after the act enforcing the Ordinance of '87, so that, during the whole pendency of the act to enforce the ordinance, the constitutional amendments were also pending.

The seventy-six members of that Congress, including sixteen of the framers of the original Constitution as before stated, were preeminently our fathers who framed that part of "the government under which we live," which is now claimed as forbidding the federal government to control slavery in the federal territories.

Is it not a little presumptuous in anyone at this day to affirm that the two things which that Congress deliberately framed, and carried to maturity at the same time, are absolutely inconsistent with each other? And does not such affirmation become impudently absurd when coupled with the other affirmation from the same mouth, that those who did the two things alleged to be inconsistent understood whether they really were inconsistent better than we, better than he who affirms that they are inconsistent?

It is surely safe to assume that the thirty-nine framers of the original Constitution, and the seventy-six members of the Congress which framed the amendments thereto, taken together do certainly include those who may be fairly called "our fathers who framed the government under which we live." And so assuming, I defy any man to show that any one of them ever, in his whole life, declared that in his understanding any proper division of local from federal authority, or any part of the Constitution, forbade the federal government to control as to slavery in the federal territories. I go a step further. I defy anyone to show that any living man in the whole world ever did, prior to the beginning of the present century (and I might almost say prior to the beginning of the last half of the present century), declare that, in his understanding, any proper division of local from federal authority, or any part of the Constitution, forbade the federal government to control as to slavery in the federal territories. To those who now so declare, I give not only "our fathers who framed the government under which we live," but with them all other living men within the century in which it was framed, among whom to search, and they shall not be able to find the evidence of a single man agreeing with them.

Now, and here, let me guard a little against being misunderstood. I do not mean to say we are bound to follow implicitly in whatever our fathers did. To do so would be to discard all the lights of current experience—to reject all progress, all improvement. What I do say is that if we would supplant the opinions and policy of our fathers in any case, we should do so upon evidence so conclusive, and argument so clear, that even their great authority, fairly considered and weighed, cannot stand, and most surely not in a case whereof we ourselves declare they understood the question better than we.

If any man at this day sincerely believes that a proper division of local from federal authority, or any part of the Constitution, forbids the federal government to control as to slavery in the federal territories, he is right to say so and to enforce his position by all truthful evidence and fair argument which he can. But he has no right to mislead others who have less access to history and less leisure to study it into the false belief that "our fathers who framed the government under which we live" were of the same opinion—thus substituting falsehood and deception for truthful evidence and fair argument. If any man at this day sincerely believes "our fathers who framed the government under which we live" used and applied principles in other cases which ought to have led them to understand that a proper division of local from federal authority or some part of the Constitution forbids the federal government to control as to slavery in the federal territories, he is right to say so. But he should, at the same time, brave the responsibility of declaring that, in his opinion, he understands their principles better than they did themselves, and especially should he not shirk that responsibility by asserting that they "understood the question just as well and even better than we do now."

But enough! Let all who believe that "our fathers who framed the government under which we live understood this question just as well and even better than we do now" speak as they spoke and act as they acted upon it. This is all Republicans ask—all Republicans desire—in relation to slavery. As those fathers marked it, so let it be again marked: as an evil not to be extended but to be tolerated and protected only because of and so far as its actual presence among us makes that toleration and protection a necessity. Let all the guarantees those fathers gave it be not grudgingly but fully and fairly maintained. For this Republicans contend, and with this, so far as I know or believe, they will be content.

And now, if they would listen—as I suppose they will not—I would address a few words to the Southern people.

I would say to them: You consider yourselves a reasonable and a just people, and I consider that in the general qualities of reason and justice you are not inferior to any other people. Still, when you speak of us Republicans, you do so only to denounce us as reptiles or, at the best, as no better than outlaws. You will grant a hearing to pirates or murderers but nothing like it to "black Republicans." In all your contentions with one another, each of you deems an unconditional condemnation of "black Republicanism" as the first thing to be attended to. Indeed, such condemnation of us seems to be an indispensable prerequisite—license, so to speak—among you to be admitted or permitted to speak at all. Now, can you or not be prevailed upon to pause and to consider whether this is quite just to us, or even to yourselves? Bring forward your charges and specifications, and then be patient long enough to hear us deny or justify.

You say we are sectional. We deny it. That makes an issue, and the burden of proof is upon you. You produce your proof, and what is it? Why, that our party has no existence in your section, gets no votes in your section. The fact is substantially true, but does it prove the issue? If it does, then in case we should, without change of principle, begin to get votes in your section, we should thereby cease to be sectional. You cannot escape this conclusion, and yet, are you willing to abide by it? If you are, you will probably soon find that we have ceased to be sectional, for we shall get votes in your section this very year. You will then begin to discover, as the truth plainly is, that your proof does not touch the issue. The fact that we get no votes in your section is a fact of your making and not of ours. And if there be fault in that fact, that fault is primarily yours and remains so until you show that we repel you by some wrong principle or practice. If we do repel you by any wrong principle or practice, the fault is ours, but this brings you to where you ought to have started—to a discussion of the right or wrong of our principle. If our principle, put in practice, would wrong your section for the benefit of ours, or for any other object, then our principle, and we with it, are sectional and are justly opposed and denounced as such. Meet us, then, on the question of whether our principle, put in practice, would wrong your section, and so meet us as if it were possible that something may be said on our side. Do you accept the challenge? No! Then you really believe that the principle which "our fathers who framed the government under which we live" thought so clearly right as to adopt it and endorse it again and again upon their official oaths, is in fact so clearly wrong as to demand your condemnation without a moment's consideration.

Some of you delight to flaunt in our faces the warning against sectional parties given by Washington in his farewell address. Less than eight years before Washington gave that warning, he had, as president of the United States, approved and signed an act of Congress enforcing the prohibition of slavery in the Northwestern Territory, which act embodied the policy of the government upon that subject up to and at the very moment he penned that warning. And about one year after he penned it, he wrote Lafayette that he considered that prohibition a wise measure, expressing in the same connection his hope that we should at some time have a confederacy of Free States.

Bearing this in mind, and seeing that sectionalism has since arisen upon this same subject, is that warning a weapon in your hands against us, or in our hands against you? Could Washington himself speak, would he cast the blame of that sectionalism upon us who sustain his policy, or upon you who repudiate it? We respect that warning of Washington, and we commend it to you, together with his example pointing to the right application of it.

But you say you are conservative—eminently conservative—while we are revolutionary, destructive, or something of the sort. What is conservatism? Is it not adherence to the old and tried against the new and untried? We stick to, contend for the identical old policy on the point in controversy which was adopted by "our fathers who framed the government under which we live," while you with one accord reject, and scout, and spit upon that old policy, and insist upon substituting something new. True, you disagree among yourselves as to what that substitute shall be. You are divided on new propositions and plans, but you are unanimous in rejecting and denouncing the old policy of the fathers. Some of you are for reviving the foreign slave trade, some for a congressional slave code for the territories, some for Congress forbidding the territories to prohibit slavery within their limits, some for maintaining slavery in the territories through the judiciary, some for the "gur-reat pur-rinciple" that "if one man would enslave another, no third man should object," fantastically called "popular sovereignty"; but never a man among you in favor of federal prohibition of slavery in federal territories, according to the practice of "our fathers who framed the government under which we live." Not one of all your various plans can show a precedent or an advocate in the century within which our government originated. Consider, then, whether your claim of conservatism for yourselves and your charge of destructiveness against us are based on the most clear and stable foundations.

Again, you say we have made the slavery question more prominent than it formerly was. We deny it. We admit that it is more prominent, but we deny that we made it so. It was not we, but you, who discarded the old policy of the fathers. We resisted, and still resist, your innovation, and thence comes the greater prominence of the question. Would you have that question reduced to its former proportions? Go back to that old policy. What has been will be again, under the same conditions. If you would have the peace of the old times, readopt the precepts and policy of the old times.

You charge that we stir up insurrections among your slaves. We deny it. And what is your proof? Harpers Ferry! John Brown!! John Brown was no Republican, and you have failed to implicate a single Republican in his Harpers Ferry enterprise. If any member of our party is guilty in that matter, you know it or you do not know it. If you do know it, you are inexcusable for not designating the man and proving the fact. If you do not know it, you are inexcusable for asserting it and especially for persisting in the assertion after you have tried and failed to make the proof. You need not be told that persisting in a charge which one does not know to be true is simply malicious slander.

Some of you admit that no Republican designedly aided or encouraged the Harpers Ferry affair but still insist that our doctrines and declarations necessarily lead to such results. We do not believe it. We know we hold to no doctrine and make no declaration which were not held to and made by "our fathers who framed the government under which we live." You never dealt fairly by us in relation to this affair. When it occurred, some important state elections were near at hand, and you were in evident glee with the belief that, by charging the blame upon us, you could get an advantage of us in those elections. The elections came, and your expectations were not quite fulfilled. Every Republican man knew that, as to himself at least, your charge was a slander, and he was not much inclined by it to cast his vote in your favor. Republican doctrines and declarations are accompanied with a continual protest against any interference whatever with your slaves or with you about your slaves. Surely this does not encourage them to revolt. True, we do, in common with "our fathers who framed the government under which we live," declare our belief that slavery is wrong, but the slaves do not hear us declare even this. For anything we say or do, the slaves would scarcely know there is a Republican Party. I believe they would not, in fact, generally know it but for your misrepresentations of us in their hearing. In your political contests among yourselves, each faction charges the other with sympathy with black Republicanism, and then, to give point to the charge, defines black Republicanism to simply be insurrection, blood and thunder among the slaves.

Slave insurrections are no more common now than they were before the Republican Party was organized. What induced the Southampton insurrection, twenty-eight years ago, in which, at least, three times as many lives were lost as at Harpers Ferry? You can scarcely stretch your very elastic fancy to the conclusion that Southampton was "got up by black Republicanism." In the present state of things in the United States, I do not think a general, or even a very extensive, slave insurrection is possible. The indispensable concert of action cannot be attained. The slaves have no means of rapid communication, nor can incendiary freemen, black or white, supply it. The explosive materials are everywhere in parcels, but there neither are, nor can be supplied, the indispensable connecting trains.

Much is said by Southern people about the affection of slaves for their masters and mistresses, and a part of it, at least, is true. A plot for an uprising could scarcely be devised and communicated to twenty individuals before some one of them, to save the life of a favorite master or mistress, would divulge it. This is the rule, and the slave revolution in Haiti was not an exception to it but a case occurring under peculiar circumstances. The gunpowder plot of British history, though not connected with slaves, was more in point. In that case, only about twenty were admitted to the secret, and yet one of them, in his anxiety to save a friend, betrayed the plot to that friend and, by consequence, averted the calamity. Occasional poisonings from the kitchen, and open or stealthy assassinations in the field, and local revolts extending to a score or so will continue to occur as the natural results of slavery, but no general insurrection of slaves, as I think, can happen in this country for a long time. Whoever much fears, or much hopes for, such an event will be alike disappointed.

In the language of Mr. Jefferson, uttered many years ago, "It is still in our power to direct the process of emancipation and deportation peaceably, and in such slow degrees as that the evil will wear off insensibly, and their places be, pari passu, filled up by free white laborers. If, on the contrary, it is left to force itself on, human nature must shudder at the prospect held up."

Mr. Jefferson did not mean to say, nor do I, that the power of emancipation is in the federal government. He spoke of

Virginia, and, as to the power of emancipation, I speak of the slaveholding states only. The federal government, however, as we insist has the power of restraining the extension of the institution—the power to ensure that a slave insurrection shall never occur on any American soil which is now free from slavery.

John Brown's effort was peculiar. It was not a slave insurrection. It was an attempt by white men to get up a revolt among slaves, in which the slaves refused to participate. In fact, it was so absurd that the slaves, with all their ignorance, saw plainly enough it could not succeed. That affair, in its philosophy, corresponds with the many attempts related in history at the assassination of kings and emperors. An enthusiast broods over the oppression of a people till he fancies himself commissioned by Heaven to liberate them. He ventures the attempt, which ends in little else than his own execution. Orsini's attempt on Louis Napoleon and John Brown's attempt at Harpers Ferry were, in their philosophy, precisely the same. The eagerness to cast blame on old England in the one case and on New England in the other does not disprove the sameness of the two things.

And how much would it avail you, if you could, by the use of John Brown, Helper's book, and the like, break up the Republican organization? Human action can be modified to some extent, but human nature cannot be changed. There is a judgment and a feeling against slavery in this nation which cast at least a million and a half of votes. You cannot destroy that judgment and feeling—that sentiment—by breaking up the political organization which rallies around it. You can scarcely scatter and disperse an army which has been formed into order in the face of your heaviest fire, but if you could, how much would you gain by forcing the sentiment which created it out of the peaceful channel of the ballot box into some other channel? What would that other channel probably be? Would the number of John Browns be lessened or enlarged by the operation?

But you will break up the union rather than submit to a denial of your constitutional rights.

That has a somewhat reckless sound, but it would be palliated, if not fully justified, were we proposing, by the mere force of numbers, to deprive you of some right plainly written down in the Constitution. But we are proposing no such thing.

When you make these declarations, you have a specific and well-understood allusion to an assumed constitutional right of yours to take slaves into the federal territories and to hold them there as property. But no such right is specifically written in the Constitution. That instrument is literally silent about any such right. We, on the contrary, deny that such a right has any existence in the Constitution, even by implication.

Your purpose, then, plainly stated, is that you will destroy the government, unless you be allowed to construe and enforce the Constitution as you please on all points in dispute between you and us. You will rule or ruin in all events.

This, plainly stated, is your language. Perhaps you will say the Supreme Court has decided the disputed constitutional question in your favor. Not quite so. But waiving the lawyer's distinction between dictum and decision, the Court have decided the question for you in a sort of way. The Court have substantially said it is your constitutional right to take slaves into the federal territories and to hold them there as property. When I say the decision was made in a sort of way, I mean it was made in a divided Court, by a bare majority of the judges, and they not quite agreeing with one another in the reasons for making it; that it is so made as that its avowed supporters disagree with one another about its meaning, and that it was mainly based upon a mistaken statement of fact—the statement in the opinion that "the right of property in a slave is distinctly and expressly affirmed in the Constitution."

An inspection of the Constitution will show that the right of property in a slave is not "distinctly and expressly affirmed" in it. Bear in mind, the judges do not pledge their judicial opinion that such right is impliedly affirmed in the Constitution, but they pledge their veracity that it is "distinctly and expressly" affirmed there—"distinctly," that is, not mingled with anything else—"expressly," that is, in words meaning just that, without the aid of any inference and susceptible of no other meaning.

If they had only pledged their judicial opinion that such right is affirmed in the instrument by implication, it would be open to others to show that neither the word "slave" nor "slavery" is to be found in the Constitution, nor the word "property" even, in any connection with language alluding to the things slave or slavery, and that wherever in that instrument the slave is alluded to, he is called a "person"—and wherever his master's legal right in relation to him is alluded to, it is spoken of as "service or labor which may be due," as a debt payable in service or labor. Also, it would be open to show, by contemporaneous history, that this mode of alluding to slaves and slavery, instead of speaking of them, was employed on purpose to exclude from the Constitution the idea that there could be property in man.

To show all this is easy and certain.

When this obvious mistake of the judges shall be brought to their notice, is it not reasonable to expect that they will withdraw the mistaken statement and reconsider the conclusion based upon it?

And then it is to be remembered that "our fathers who framed the government under which we live"—the men who made the Constitution—decided this same constitutional question in our favor long ago—decided it without division among themselves when making the decision, without division among themselves about the meaning of it after it was made, and, so far as any evidence is left, without basing it upon any mistaken statement of facts.

Under all these circumstances, do you really feel yourselves justified to break up this government, unless such a court decision as yours is shall be at once submitted to as a conclusive and final rule of political action? But you will not abide the election of a Republican president! In that supposed event, you say, you will destroy the union, and then, you say, the great crime of having destroyed it will be upon us! That is cool. A highwayman holds a pistol to my ear and mutters through his teeth, "Stand and deliver, or I shall kill you, and then you will be a murderer!"

To be sure, what the robber demanded of me—my money—was my own, and I had a clear right to keep it, but it was no more my own than my vote is my own, and the threat of death to me, to extort my money, and the threat of destruction to the union, to extort my vote, can scarcely be distinguished in principle.

A few words now to Republicans. It is exceedingly desirable that all parts of this great confederacy shall be at peace and in harmony one with another. Let us Republicans do our part to have it so. Even though much provoked, let us do nothing through passion and ill temper. Even though the Southern people will not so much as listen to us, let us calmly consider their demands and yield to them if, in our deliberate view of our duty, we possibly can. Judging by all they say and do, and by the subject and nature of their controversy with us, let us determine, if we can, what will satisfy them.

Will they be satisfied if the territories be unconditionally surrendered to them? We know they will not. In all their present complaints against us, the territories are scarcely mentioned. Invasions and insurrections are the rage now. Will it satisfy them if, in the future, we have nothing to do with invasions and insurrections? We know it will not. We so know because we know we never had anything to do with invasions and insurrections, and yet this total abstaining does not exempt us from the charge and the denunciation.

The question recurs, what will satisfy them? Simply this: We must not only let them alone, but we must, somehow, convince them that we do let them alone. This, we know by experience, is no easy task. We have been so trying to convince them from the very beginning of our organization, but with no success. In all our platforms and speeches we have constantly protested our purpose to let them alone, but this has had no tendency to convince them. Alike unavailing to convince them is the fact that they have never detected a man of us in any attempt to disturb them.

These natural, and apparently adequate, means all failing, what will convince them? This, and this only: cease to call slavery wrong and join them in calling it right. And this must be done thoroughly—done in acts as well as in words. Silence will not be tolerated; we must place ourselves avowedly with them. Senator Douglas's new sedition law must be enacted and enforced, suppressing all declarations that slavery is wrong, whether made in politics, in presses, in pulpits, or in private. We must arrest and return their fugitive slaves with greedy pleasure. We must pull down our Free State constitutions. The whole atmosphere must be disinfected from all taint of opposition to slavery before they will cease to believe that all their troubles proceed from us.

I am quite aware they do not state their case precisely in this way. Most of them would probably say to us, "Let us alone, do nothing to us, and say what you please about slavery." But we do let them alone—have never disturbed them—so that, after all, it is what we say which dissatisfies them. They will continue to accuse us of doing until we cease saying.

I am also aware they have not as yet in terms demanded the overthrow of our Free State constitutions. Yet those constitutions declare the wrong of slavery with more solemn emphasis than do all other sayings against it. And when all these other sayings shall have been silenced, the overthrow of these constitutions will be demanded and nothing be left to resist the demand. It is nothing to the contrary that they do not demand the whole of this just now. Demanding what they do, and for the reason they do, they can voluntarily stop nowhere short of this consummation. Holding, as they do, that slavery is morally right and socially elevating, they cannot cease to demand a full national recognition of it as a legal right and a social blessing.

Nor can we justifiably withhold this on any ground save our conviction that slavery is wrong. If slavery is right, all words, acts, laws, and constitutions against it are themselves wrong and should be silenced and swept away. If it is right, we cannot justly object to its nationality—its universality; if it is wrong, they cannot justly insist upon its extension—its enlargement. All they ask, we could readily grant if we thought slavery right; all we ask, they could as readily grant if they thought it wrong. Their thinking it right and our thinking it wrong is the precise fact upon which depends the whole controversy. Thinking it right, as they do, they are not to blame for desiring its full recognition as being right; but thinking it wrong, as we do, can we yield to them? Can we cast our votes with their view and against our own? In view of our moral, social, and political responsibilities, can we do this?

Wrong as we think slavery is, we can yet afford to let it alone where it is, because that much is due to the necessity arising from its actual presence in the nation. But can we, while our votes will prevent it, allow it to spread into the national territories and to overrun us here in these Free States? If our sense of duty forbids this, then let us stand by our duty fearlessly and effectively. Let us be diverted by none of those sophistical contrivances wherewith we are so industriously plied and belabored—contrivances such as groping for some middle ground between the right and the wrong, vain as the search for a man who should be neither a living man nor a dead man—such as a policy of "don't care" on a question about which all true men do care—such as union appeals beseeching true union men to yield to disunionists, reversing the divine rule, and calling not the sinners but the righteous to repentance—such as invocations to Washington, imploring men to unsay what Washington said and undo what Washington did.

Neither let us be slandered from our duty by false accusations against us nor frightened from it by menaces of destruction to the government nor of dungeons to ourselves. LET US HAVE FAITH THAT RIGHT MAKES MIGHT, AND IN THAT FAITH, LET US, TO THE END, DARE TO DO OUR DUTY AS WE UNDERSTAND IT.

13

Speech at Independence Hall, Philadelphia, Pennsylvania

February 22, 1861

Giving speeches along his route to Washington for his inauguration ten days hence, Lincoln was careful to say nothing to provoke the anger of rebellious Southerners. Shortly after Lincoln's
election as president, in December 1860 South Carolina seceded
from the union, and six states soon followed. On February 18,
four days before this speech, Jefferson Davis was elected president of the Confederate States of America. At Independence
Hall, however, Lincoln could not resist provocation. The Declaration of Independence was a matter of contention for Confederates who denounced the notion that all men are created equal,
but Lincoln uses the symbolism of the signing place of the Declaration to call for patriotism and devotion to principle. Bittersweet
in light of his eventual assassination are Lincoln's words about
what he was willing to live and die for.

[UNABRIDGED]
Address in Independence Hall

Mr. Cuyler:

I am filled with deep emotion at finding myself standing
here, in this place, where were collected together the wisdom,
the patriotism, the devotion to principle from which sprang
the institutions under which we live. You have kindly suggested to me that in my hands is the task of restoring peace to

the present distracted condition of the country. I can say in return, sir, that all the political sentiments I entertain have been drawn, so far as I have been able to draw them, from the sentiments which originated and were given to the world from this hall in which we stand. I have never had a feeling politically that did not spring from the sentiments embodied in the Declaration of Independence. I have often pondered over the dangers which were incurred by the men who assembled here and framed and adopted that Declaration of Independence. I have pondered over the toils that were endured by the officers and soldiers of the army who achieved that independence. I have often inquired of myself what great principle or idea it was that kept this confederacy so long together. It was not the mere matter of the separation of the colonies from the motherland but that sentiment in the Declaration of Independence which gave liberty not alone to the people of this country but, I hope, to the world, for all future time. It was that which gave promise that in due time the weights would be lifted from the shoulders of all men. This is a sentiment embodied in the Declaration of Independence. Now, my friends, can this country be saved upon that basis? If it can, I will consider myself one of the happiest men in the world if I can help to save it. If it cannot be saved upon that principle, it will be truly awful. But if this country cannot be saved without giving up that principle, I was about to say I would rather be assassinated on this spot than surrender it.

Now, in my view of the present aspect of affairs, there need be no bloodshed and war. There is no necessity for it. I am not in favor of such a course, and I may say, in advance, that there will be no bloodshed unless it be forced upon the government, and then it will be compelled to act in self-defense.

My friends, this is wholly an unprepared speech, and I did

not expect to be called upon to say a word when I came here. I supposed it was merely to do something toward raising the flag. I may, therefore, have said something indiscreet. [Cries of "No, no."] I have said nothing but what I am willing to live by and, if it be the pleasure of Almighty God, die by.

14

First Inaugural Address

March 4, 1861

Abraham Lincoln's inaugural address, given on March 4, 1861, pleads for rationality and calm. While using contract law as well as the Constitution and the Declaration of Independence to prove the illegality of secession, he strives to allay fears that his party aimed at dismantling slavery. The presidency conveyed no such power, he asserts, and the Supreme Court of Chief Justice Roger Taney had interpreted the Constitution to permit no such meddling. The rule of law constrained him no less than he expects it to constrain his fellow Americans. He pleads with the seceding states to reconsider their rash actions. In only another four years, he points out, those dissatisfied might elect a president more to their liking. For all his rational argument, for all his emotional appeals—which borders on begging—Lincoln's first inaugural address has an iron lining. It makes clear his underlying, nonnegotiable premise that the union is perpetual, and he would defend it against disruption.

[ABRIDGED]

... Apprehension seems to exist among the people of the Southern states that by the accession of a Republican administration, their property and their peace and personal security are to be endangered. There has never been any reasonable cause for such apprehension. Indeed, the most ample evidence to the contrary has all the while existed and been open to their inspection. It is found in nearly all the published speeches of him who now addresses you.

I do but quote from one of those speeches when I declare that "I have no purpose, directly or indirectly, to interfere with the institution of slavery in the states where it exists. I believe I have no lawful right to do so, and I have no inclination to do so." Those who nominated and elected me did so with full knowledge that I had made this and many similar declarations and had never recanted them. And more than this, they placed in the platform, for my acceptance and as a law to themselves and to me, the clear and emphatic resolution which I now read:

"Resolved, that the maintenance inviolate of the rights of the states, and especially the right of each state to order and control its own domestic institutions according to its own judgment exclusively, is essential to that balance of power on which the perfection and endurance of our political fabric depend; and we denounce the lawless invasion by armed force of the soil of any state or territory, no matter under what pretext, as among the gravest of crimes."

I now reiterate these sentiments, and in doing so, I only press upon the public attention the most conclusive evidence of which the case is susceptible, that the property, peace, and security of no section are to be in anywise endangered by the now incoming administration. I add too that all the protection which, consistently with the Constitution and the laws, can be given will be cheerfully given to all the states when lawfully demanded, for whatever cause—as cheerfully to one section as to another . . .

I take the official oath today with no mental reservations and with no purpose to construe the Constitution or laws by any hypercritical rules. And while I do not choose now to specify particular acts of Congress as proper to be enforced, I do suggest that it will be much safer for all, both in official and private stations, to conform to and abide by all those acts which stand unrepealed than to violate any of them, trusting to find impunity in having them held to be unconstitutional.

It is seventy-two years since the first inauguration of a president under our national Constitution. During that period fifteen different and greatly distinguished citizens have, in succession, administered the executive branch of the government. They have conducted it through many perils and, generally, with great success. Yet, with all this scope for precedent, I now enter upon the same task for the brief constitutional term of four years under great and peculiar difficulty. A disruption of the federal union heretofore only menaced is now formidably attempted.

I hold that in contemplation of universal law, and of the Constitution, the union of these states is perpetual. Perpetuity is implied, if not expressed, in the fundamental law of all national governments. It is safe to assert that no government proper ever had a provision in its organic law for its own termination. Continue to execute all the express provisions of our national Constitution, and the union will endure forever—it being impossible to destroy it except by some action not provided for in the instrument itself.

Again, if the United States be not a government proper, but an association of states in the nature of contract merely, can it, as a contract, be peaceably unmade by less than all the parties who made it? One party to a contract may violate it—break it, so to speak—but does it not require all to lawfully rescind it?

Descending from these general principles, we find the proposition that in legal contemplation the union is perpetual confirmed by the history of the union itself. The union is much older than the Constitution. It was formed, in fact, by the Articles of Association in 1774. It was matured and continued by the Declaration of Independence in 1776. It was further matured, and the faith of all the then thirteen states expressly plighted and engaged that it should be perpetual, by the Articles of Confederation in 1778. And finally, in 1787, one of the declared objects for ordaining and establishing the Constitution was "to form a more perfect union." . . .

I therefore consider that in view of the Constitution and the laws, the union is unbroken, and, to the extent of my ability, I shall take care, as the Constitution itself expressly enjoins upon me, that the laws of the union be faithfully executed in all the states. Doing this I deem to be only a simple duty on my part, and I shall perform it, so far as practicable, unless my rightful masters, the American people, shall withhold the requisite means or, in some authoritative manner, direct the contrary. I trust this will not be regarded as a menace but only as the declared purpose of the union that it will constitutionally defend and maintain itself.

In doing this there needs to be no bloodshed or violence; and there shall be none, unless it be forced upon the national authority . . .

That there are persons in one section or another who seek to destroy the union at all events, and are glad of any pretext to do it, I will neither affirm or deny. But if there be such, I need address no word to them. To those, however, who really love the union, may I not speak?

Before entering upon so grave a matter as the destruction of our national fabric, with all its benefits, its memories, and its hopes, would it not be wise to ascertain precisely why we do it? Will you hazard so desperate a step while there is any possibility that any portion of the ills you fly from have no real existence? Will you, while the certain ills you fly to are greater than all the real ones you fly from? Will you risk the commission of so fearful a mistake?

All profess to be content in the union if all constitutional rights can be maintained. Is it true, then, that any right plainly written in the Constitution has been denied? I think not. Happily the human mind is so constituted that no party can reach to the audacity of doing this. Think, if you can, of a single instance in which a plainly written provision of the Constitution has ever been denied. If, by the mere force of numbers, a majority should deprive a minority of any clearly written constitutional right, it might, in a moral point of view, justify revolution—certainly would if such right were a vital one. But such is not our case. All the vital rights of minorities, and of individuals, are so plainly assured to them by affirmations and negations, guarantees and prohibitions in the Constitution that controversies never arise concerning them. But no organic law can ever be framed with a provision specifically applicable to every question which may occur in practical administration. No foresight can anticipate nor any document of reasonable length contain express provisions for all possible questions. Shall fugitives from labor be surrendered by national or by state authority? The Constitution does not expressly say. May Congress prohibit slavery in the territories? The Constitution does not expressly say. Must Congress protect slavery in the territories? The Constitution does not expressly say.

From questions of this class spring all our constitutional controversies, and we divide upon them into majorities and minorities. If the minority will not acquiesce, the majority must, or the government must cease. There is no other alternative; for continuing the government is acquiescence on one side or the other. If a minority in such case will secede rather than acquiesce, they make a precedent which, in turn, will divide and ruin them; for a minority of their own will secede from them whenever a majority refuses to be controlled by such minority. For instance, why may not any portion of a new confederacy, a year or two hence, arbitrarily secede again, precisely as portions of the present union now claim to secede from it. All who cherish disunion sentiments are now being educated to the exact temper of doing this. Is there such perfect identity of interests among the states to compose a new union as to produce harmony only and prevent renewed secession?

Plainly, the central idea of secession is the essence of anarchy. A majority, held in restraint by constitutional checks and limitations, and always changing easily with deliberate changes of popular opinions and sentiments, is the only true sovereign of a free people. Whoever rejects it does, of necessity, fly to anarchy or to despotism. Unanimity is impossible; the rule of a minority, as a permanent arrangement, is wholly inadmissible; so that, rejecting the majority principle, anarchy or despotism in some form is all that is left.

I do not forget the position assumed by some that constitutional questions are to be decided by the Supreme Court. Nor do I deny that such decisions must be binding in any case upon the parties to a suit as to the object of that suit, while they are also entitled to very high respect and consideration in all parallel cases by all other departments of the government. And while it is obviously possible that such decision may be erroneous in any given case, still the evil effect following it, being limited to that particular case, with the chance that it may be overruled and never become a precedent for other cases, can better be borne than could the evils of a different practice. At the same time, the candid citizen must confess that if the policy of the government upon vital questions affecting the whole people is to be irrevocably fixed by decisions of the Supreme Court the instant they are made, in ordinary litigation between parties, in personal actions, the people will have ceased to be their own rulers, having, to that extent, practically resigned their government into the hands of that eminent tribunal . . .

One section of our country believes slavery is right and ought to be extended, while the other believes it is wrong and ought not to be extended. This is the only substantial dispute. The fugitive slave clause of the Constitution and the law for the suppression of the foreign slave trade are each as well enforced, perhaps, as any law can ever be in a community where the moral sense of the people imperfectly supports the law itself. The great body of the people abide by the dry legal obligation in both cases, and a few break over in each. This, I think, cannot be perfectly cured, and it would be worse in both cases after the separation of the sections than before. The foreign slave trade, now imperfectly suppressed, would be ultimately revived without restriction in one section, while fugitive slaves, now only partially surrendered, would not be surrendered at all by the other.

Physically speaking, we cannot separate. We cannot remove our respective sections from each other nor build an impassable wall between them. A husband and wife may be divorced, and go out of the presence and beyond the reach of each other, but the different parts of our country cannot do this. They cannot but remain face-to-face, and intercourse, either amicable or hostile, must continue between them. Is it possible then to make that intercourse more advantageous, or more satisfactory, after separation than before? Can aliens make treaties easier than friends can make laws? Can treaties be more faithfully enforced between aliens than laws can among friends? Suppose you go to war. You cannot fight always, and when, after much loss on both sides and no gain on either, you cease fighting, the identical old questions as to terms of intercourse are again upon you.

This country, with its institutions, belongs to the people who inhabit it. Whenever they shall grow weary of the existing government, they can exercise their constitutional right of amending it, or their revolutionary right to dismember or overthrow it. I cannot be ignorant of the fact that many worthy and patriotic citizens are desirous of having the national Constitution amended. While I make no recommendation of amendments, I fully recognize the rightful authority of the people over the whole subject, to be exercised in either of the modes prescribed in the instrument itself, and I should, under existing circumstances, favor rather than oppose a fair opportunity being afforded the people to act upon it . . .

The chief magistrate derives all his authority from the people, and they have conferred none upon him to fix terms for the separation of the states. The people themselves can do this also if they choose, but the executive, as such, has nothing to do with it. His duty is to administer the present government as it came to his hands and to transmit it, unimpaired by him, to his successor.

Why should there not be a patient confidence in the ultimate justice of the people? Is there any better, or equal, hope in the world? In our present differences, is either party without faith of being in the right? If the Almighty Ruler of nations, with His eternal truth and justice, be on your side of the North, or on yours of the South, that truth, and that justice, will surely prevail by the judgment of this great tribunal, the American people.

By the frame of the government under which we live, this same people have wisely given their public servants but little power for mischief, and have, with equal wisdom, provided for the return of that little to their own hands at very short intervals.

While the people retain their virtue and vigilance, no administration, by any extreme of wickedness or folly, can very seriously injure the government in the short space of four years.

My countrymen, one and all, think calmly and well upon this whole subject. Nothing valuable can be lost by taking time. If there be an object to hurry any of you, in hot haste, to a step which you would never take deliberately, that object will be frustrated by taking time, but no good object can be frustrated by it. Such of you as are now dissatisfied still have the old Constitution unimpaired and, on the sensitive point, the laws of your own framing under it, while the new administration will have no immediate power, if it would, to change either. If it were admitted that you who are dissatisfied hold the right side in the dispute, there still is no single good reason for precipitate action. Intelligence, patriotism, Christianity, and a firm reliance on Him, who has never yet forsaken this favored land, are still competent to adjust, in the best way, all our present difficulty.

In your hands, my dissatisfied fellow countrymen, and not in mine is the momentous issue of civil war. The government will not assail you. You can have no conflict without being yourselves the aggressors. You have no oath registered in Heaven to destroy the government, while I shall have the most solemn one to "preserve, protect and defend" it.

I am loath to close. We are not enemies but friends. We must not be enemies. Though passion may have strained, it must not break our bonds of affection. The mystic chords of memory, stretching from every battlefield and patriot grave to every living heart and hearthstone all over this broad land, will yet swell the chorus of the union when again touched, as surely they will be, by the better angels of our nature.

15

Message to Congress in Special Session

July 4, 1861

At this special session of Congress, which had not been scheduled to meet in regular session until December, Lincoln summa-
rizes the Confederate attack on Fort Sumter on April 12 and the
steps now needed to defend the union. The following excerpt
concludes this report to Congress and shows Lincoln's faith in the
common man and his determination to keep the American experiment of democracy alive.

[ABRIDGED]

... That this was their object, the executive well understood,
and having said to them in the inaugural address, "You can
have no conflict without being yourselves the aggressors," he
took pains not only to keep this declaration good but also to
keep the case so free from the power of ingenious sophistry as
that the world should not be able to misunderstand it. By the
affair at Fort Sumter, with its surrounding circumstances, that
point was reached. Then, and thereby, the assailants of the
government began the conflict of arms, without a gun in sight
or in expectancy to return their fire, save only the few in the
fort sent to that harbor years before for their own protection
and still ready to give that protection in whatever was lawful.
In this act, discarding all else, they have forced upon the
country the distinct issue: "immediate dissolution, or blood."

And this issue embraces more than the fate of these United States. It presents to the whole family of man the question whether a constitutional republic or a democracy—a government of the people, by the same people—can or cannot maintain its territorial integrity against its own domestic foes. It presents the question whether discontented individuals, too few in numbers to control administration, according to organic law, in any case, can always, upon the pretenses made in this case, or on any other pretenses, or arbitrarily, without any pretense, break up their government and thus practically put an end to free government upon the earth. It forces us to ask: "Is there, in all republics, this inherent and fatal weakness?" "Must a government of necessity be too strong for the liberties of its own people, or too weak to maintain its own existence?"

So viewing the issue, no choice was left but to call out the war power of the government and so to resist force employed for its destruction by force for its preservation . . .

It may well be questioned whether there is today a majority of the legally qualified voters of any state, except perhaps South Carolina, in favor of disunion. There is much reason to believe that the union men are the majority in many if not in every other one of the so-called seceded states. The contrary has not been demonstrated in any one of them. It is ventured to affirm this, even of Virginia and Tennessee, for the result of an election held in military camps, where the bayonets are all on one side of the question voted upon, can scarcely be considered as demonstrating popular sentiment. At such an election, all that large class who are, at once, for the union and against coercion would be coerced to vote against the union.

It may be affirmed, without extravagance, that the free institutions we enjoy have developed the powers and improved the condition of our whole people beyond any example in the world. Of this we now have a striking and an impressive illustration. So large an army as the government has now on foot was never before known without a soldier in it but who had taken his place there of his own free choice. But more than this: There are many single regiments whose members, one and another, possess full practical knowledge of all the arts, sciences, professions, and whatever else, whether useful or elegant, is known in the world, and there is scarcely one from which there could not be selected a president, a cabinet, a congress, and perhaps a court abundantly competent to administer the government itself. Nor do I say this is not true, also, in the army of our late friends, now adversaries, in this contest. But if it is, so much better the reason why the government, which has conferred such benefits on both them and us, should not be broken up. Whoever, in any section, proposes to abandon such a government would do well to consider, in deference to what principle it is that he does it, what better he is likely to get in its stead—whether the substitute will give, or be intended to give, so much of good to the people. There are some foreshadowings on this subject. Our adversaries have adopted some declarations of independence, in which, unlike the good old one penned by Jefferson, they omit the words "all men are created equal." Why? They have adopted a temporary national constitution, in the preamble of which, unlike our good old one signed by Washington, they omit "We, the people" and substitute "We, the deputies of the sovereign and independent states." Why? Why this deliberate pressing out of view the rights of men and the authority of the people?

This is essentially a people's contest. On the side of the union, it is a struggle for maintaining in the world that form and substance of government whose leading object is to elevate the condition of men—to lift artificial weights from all shoulders—to clear the paths of laudable pursuit for all—to afford all an unfettered start and a fair chance in the race of life. Yielding to partial and temporary departures from necessity, this is the leading object of the government for whose existence we contend.

I am most happy to believe that the plain people understand and appreciate this. It is worthy of note that while in this, the government's hour of trial, large numbers of those in the army and navy who have been favored with the offices have resigned and proved false to the hand which had pampered them, not one common soldier or common sailor is known to have deserted his flag . . .

Our popular government has often been called an experiment. Two points in it our people have already settled: the successful establishing and the successful administering of it. One still remains: its successful maintenance against a formidable attempt to overthrow it. It is now for them to demonstrate to the world that those who can fairly carry an election can also suppress a rebellion—that ballots are the rightful and peaceful successors of bullets, and that when ballots have fairly and constitutionally decided, there can be no successful appeal back to bullets, that there can be no successful appeal except to ballots themselves at succeeding elections. Such will be a great lesson of peace: teaching men that what they cannot take by an election, neither can they take it by a war— teaching all the folly of being the beginners of a war.

Lest there be some uneasiness in the minds of candid men as to what is to be the course of the government toward the Southern states after the rebellion shall have been suppressed, the executive deems it proper to say it will be his purpose then, as ever, to be guided by the Constitution and the laws, and that he probably will have no different understanding of the powers and duties of the federal government, relatively to the rights of the states and the people under the Constitution, than that expressed in the inaugural address . . .

It was with the deepest regret that the executive found the duty of employing the war power, in defense of the government, forced upon him. He could but perform this duty or surrender the existence of the government. No compromise by public servants could, in this case, be a cure; not that compromises are not often proper, but that no popular government can long survive a marked precedent that those who carry an election can only save the government from immediate destruction by giving up the main point upon which the people gave the election. The people themselves, and not their servants, can safely reverse their own deliberate decisions. As a private citizen, the executive could not have consented that these institutions shall perish; much less could he in betrayal of so vast and so sacred a trust as these free people had confided to him. He felt that he had no moral right to shrink nor even to count the chances of his own life in what might follow. In full view of his great responsibility, he has, so far, done what he has deemed his duty. You will now, according to your own judgment, perform yours. He sincerely hopes that your views and your action may so accord with his as to assure all faithful citizens who have been disturbed in their rights of a certain and speedy restoration to them, under the Constitution and the laws.

And having thus chosen our course, without guile and with pure purpose, let us renew our trust in God and go forward without fear and with manly hearts.

ABRAHAM LINCOLN

16

Annual Message to Congress

December 3, 1861

Required by the Constitution, the "Annual Message to Congress" (now referred to as the State of the Union address) tends to include an assessment of the financial situation, the need for particular legislative action, relations with other countries, etc. In addition, Lincoln reported on the eight months of the raging Civil War.

Regarding developments with foreign nations, Lincoln is optimistic about nonintervention by European powers. He then recommends that the United States recognize "the independence and sovereignty of Haiti and Liberia." His statement that he was unable to discern any reason to the contrary is classic Lincoln understatement; he knew the only reason the two countries had not been recognized is that they were black governed.

In another excerpt reproduced here, Lincoln discusses a law passed by Congress titled "An act to confiscate property used for insurrectionary purposes," in other words, freeing Southern enslaved workers. Lincoln proposes colonization.

The last excerpt is reminiscent of his address to the Wisconsin State Agricultural Society in September 1859. This remarkable analysis of labor and capital exemplifies Lincoln's insistence that American democracy means open opportunity for all.

... If any good reason exists why we should persevere longer in withholding our recognition of the independence and sovereignty of Haiti and Liberia, I am unable to discern it. Unwilling, however, to inaugurate a novel policy in regard to them without the approbation of Congress, I submit for your consideration the expediency of an appropriation for maintaining a chargé d'affaires near each of those new states. It ... does not admit of doubt that important commercial advantages might be secured by favorable commercial treaties with them ...

Under and by virtue of the act of Congress entitled "An act to confiscate property used for insurrectionary purposes," approved August 6, 1861, the legal claims of certain persons to the labor and service of certain other persons have become forfeited, and numbers of the latter, thus liberated, are already dependent on the United States and must be provided for in some way. Besides this, it is not impossible that some of the states will pass similar enactments for their own benefit respectively, and by operation of which persons of the same class will be thrown upon them for disposal. In such case I recommend that Congress provide for accepting such persons from such states, according to some mode of valuation, in lieu, *pro tanto*, of direct taxes, or upon some other plan to be agreed on with such states respectively; that such persons, on such acceptance by the general government, be at once deemed free; and that, in any event, steps be taken for colonizing both classes (or the one first mentioned, if the other shall not be brought into existence) at some place or places in a climate congenial to them. It might be well to consider too whether the free colored people already in the United States could not, so far as individuals may desire, be included in such colonization ...

It continues to develop that the insurrection is largely, if not exclusively, a war upon the first principle of popular government—the rights of the people. Conclusive evidence of this is found in the most grave and maturely considered public documents, as well as in the general tone of the insurgents. In those documents we find the abridgment of the existing right of suffrage and the denial to the people of all right to participate in the selection of public officers except the legislative, boldly advocated with labored arguments to prove that large control of the people in government is the source of all political evil. Monarchy itself is sometimes hinted at as a possible refuge from the power of the people.

In my present position, I could scarcely be justified were I to omit raising a warning voice against this approach of returning despotism.

It is not needed, nor fitting here, that a general argument should be made in favor of popular institutions, but there is one point, with its connections not so hackneyed as most others, to which I ask a brief attention. It is the effort to place capital on an equal footing with, if not above, labor in the structure of government. It is assumed that labor is available only in connection with capital, that nobody labors unless somebody else, owning capital, somehow by the use of it induces him to labor. This assumed, it is next considered whether it is best that capital shall hire laborers and thus induce them to work by their own consent, or buy them and drive them to it without their consent. Having proceeded so far, it is naturally concluded that all laborers are either hired laborers or what we call slaves. And further it is assumed that whoever is once a hired laborer is fixed in that condition for life.

Now, there is no such relation between capital and labor as assumed, nor is there any such thing as a freeman being fixed for life in the condition of a hired laborer. Both these assumptions are false, and all inferences from them are groundless.

Labor is prior to, and independent of, capital. Capital is only the fruit of labor and could never have existed if labor had not first existed. Labor is the superior of capital and deserves much the higher consideration. Capital has its rights, which are as worthy of protection as any other rights. Nor is it denied that there is, and probably always will be, a relation between labor and capital producing mutual benefits. The error is in assuming that the whole labor of community exists within that relation. A few men own capital, and that few avoid labor themselves and, with their capital, hire or buy another few to labor for them. A large majority belong to neither class—neither work for others nor have others working for them. In most of the Southern states, a majority of the whole people of all colors are neither slaves nor masters, while in the Northern a large majority are neither hirers nor hired. Men with their families—wives, sons, and daughters—work for themselves, on their farms, in their houses, and in their shops, taking the whole product to themselves and asking no favors of capital on the one hand nor of hired laborers or slaves on the other. It is not forgotten that a considerable number of persons mingle their own labor with capital—that is, they labor with their own hands and also buy or hire others to labor for them—but this is only a mixed and not a distinct class. No principle stated is disturbed by the existence of this mixed class.

Again, as has already been said, there is not of necessity any such thing as the free hired laborer being fixed to that condition for life. Many independent men everywhere in these states a few years back in their lives were hired laborers. The prudent, penniless beginner in the world labors for wages awhile, saves a surplus with which to buy tools or land for himself, then labors on his own account another while, and at length hires another new beginner to help him. This is the just, and generous, and prosperous system, which opens the way to all—gives hope to all, and consequent energy, and progress, and improvement of condition to all. No men living are more worthy to be trusted than those who toil up from poverty, none less inclined to take or touch aught which they have not honestly earned. Let them beware of surrendering a political power which they already possess and which, if surrendered, will surely be used to close the door of advancement against such as they and to fix new disabilities and burdens upon them, till all of liberty shall be lost.

. . . The struggle of today is not altogether for today—it is for a vast future also. With a reliance on Providence, all the more firm and earnest, let us proceed in the great task which events have devolved upon us.

ABRAHAM LINCOLN

17

Letter to Horace Greeley

August 22, 1862

On August 19, 1862, Horace Greeley, editor of the *New-York Tribune* and a founding member of the Republican Party, wrote a lengthy editorial criticizing Lincoln's policy regarding slavery. In the form of a letter to the president titled "The Prayer of Twenty Millions," Greeley declared that the majority of Northerners favored immediate abolition and were "sorely disappointed and deeply pained" by Lincoln's policy on slavery. But Lincoln knew otherwise; the people, and the fighting soldiers, favored saving the union, not ending slavery. The irony is that Lincoln, on July 22, 1862, had already secretly presented to his cabinet his plans for emancipation. Lincoln's response to Greeley is a brilliant political stance. Greeley's disparagement actually offered Lincoln an opportunity to calm conservative fears while paving a way forward. Portions of this letter are often quoted as a tactic to prove that Lincoln did not truly care about slavery. This tactic, however, always omits the context as well as the essential concluding sentence.

Executive Mansion, Washington
Hon. Horace Greeley

Dear Sir

I have just read yours of the 19th addressed to myself through the *New-York Tribune*. If there be in it any statements or assumptions of fact which I may know to be erroneous, I do not, now and here, controvert them. If there be in it any inferences which I may believe to be falsely drawn, I do not, now and here, argue against them. If there be perceptible in it an impatient and dictatorial tone, I waive it in deference to an old friend whose heart I have always supposed to be right.

As to the policy I "seem to be pursuing," as you say, I have not meant to leave anyone in doubt.

I would save the union. I would save it the shortest way under the Constitution. The sooner the national authority can be restored, the nearer the union will be "the union as it was." If there be those who would not save the union unless they could at the same time save slavery, I do not agree with them. If there be those who would not save the union unless they could at the same time destroy slavery, I do not agree with them. My paramount object in this struggle is to save the union, and is not either to save or to destroy slavery. If I could save the union without freeing any slave I would do it, and if I could save it by freeing all the slaves I would do it, and if I could save it by freeing some and leaving others alone I would also do that. What I do about slavery, and the colored race, I do because I believe it helps to save the union; and what I forbear, I forbear because I do not believe it would help to save the union. I shall do less whenever I shall believe what I am doing hurts the cause, and I shall do more whenever I shall believe doing more will help the cause. I shall try to correct errors when shown to be errors, and I shall adopt new views so fast as they shall appear to be true views.

I have here stated my purpose according to my view of official duty, and I intend no modification of my oft-expressed personal wish that all men everywhere could be free.

Yours,

A. LINCOLN

18

Letter to Fanny McCullough

December 23, 1862

Killed in battle in Mississippi on December 5, 1862, Lieutenant Colonel William McCullough had been clerk of the McLean County Circuit Court in Bloomington, Illinois, and was a friend of Lincoln's. Amid the horrors of war, Lincoln takes the time to write a sympathy letter to McCullough's grieving daughter Fanny. This poignant and endearing letter exemplifies Lincoln's capacity for compassion not only for children but for all the loved ones of the six hundred thousand Union and Confederate soldiers who died in the war.

[UNABRIDGED]

Executive Mansion, Washington

Dear Fanny

It is with deep grief that I learn of the death of your kind and brave father and, especially, that it is affecting your young heart beyond what is common in such cases. In this sad world of ours, sorrow comes to all; and, to the young, it comes with bitterest agony because it takes them unawares. The older have learned to ever expect it. I am anxious to afford some alleviation of your present distress. Perfect relief is not possible, except with time. You cannot now realize that you will ever feel better. Is not this so? And yet it is a mistake. You are sure to be happy again. To know this, which is certainly true, will make you some less miserable now. I have had experience enough to know what I say, and you need only to believe it to feel better at once. The memory of your dear father, instead of an agony, will yet be a sad sweet feeling in your heart of a purer and holier sort than you have known before.

Please present my kind regards to your afflicted mother.

Your sincere friend A. LINCOLN.

19

Emancipation Proclamation

January 1, 1863

On July 22, 1862, Lincoln told his cabinet that he had decided to issue an emancipation proclamation. Grappling with the issue of the rule of law and his power under the Constitution, Lincoln believed he could issue the proclamation only as a war measure. For that reason his language is legalistic rather than poetical. Emancipation took effect on New Year's Day, 1863. While the proclamation was not effective in Confederate states because the U.S. Army was not in position to enforce it, and while it did not cover enslaved workers held by loyal slaveholders in the Union border states, the end of slavery was now United States policy. The proclamation also called for allowing African Americans to serve in the Union armed services at a time when manpower needs were critical. Fully two hundred thousand African American men mustered into federal service over the next two years.

To Southerners, the most threatening part of the proclamation was Union-sanctioned slave rebellion: Governmental authority "will do no act or acts to repress such person, or any of them, in any efforts they may make for their actual freedom." The document recommended that the people continue peacefully to work for wages and that they "abstain from all violence," but— previously unheard of in U.S. race relations—that admonition against violence did not include "necessary self-defense."

The measure clarified a moral issue: The war for the union was now undeniably a war for freedom. Although it would take victory and the Thirteenth Amendment to make it official nation-wide, the definition of America was transformed.

[ABRIDGED]
Emancipation Proclamation
By the President of the United States of America:
A Proclamation.

Whereas, on the twenty-second day of September, in the year of our Lord one thousand eight hundred and sixty-two, a proclamation was issued by the president of the United States, containing, among other things, the following, to wit:

"That on the first day of January, in the year of our Lord one thousand eight hundred and sixty-three, all persons held as slaves within any state or designated part of a state the people whereof shall then be in rebellion against the United States, shall be then, thenceforward, and forever free; and the executive government of the United States, including the military and naval authority thereof, will recognize and maintain the freedom of such persons and will do no act or acts to repress such persons, or any of them, in any efforts they may make for their actual freedom.

"That the executive will, on the first day of January aforesaid, by proclamation designate the states and parts of states, if any, in which the people thereof, respectively, shall then be in rebellion against the United States, and the fact that any state, or the people thereof, shall on that day be, in good faith, represented in the Congress of the United States by members chosen thereto at elections wherein a majority of the qualified voters of such state shall have participated, shall, in the absence of strong countervailing testimony, be deemed conclusive evidence that such state, and the people thereof, are not then in rebellion against the United States."

Now, therefore I, Abraham Lincoln, president of the United States, by virtue of the power in me vested as commander in chief of the Army and Navy of the United States in time of actual armed rebellion against authority and government of the United States, and as a fit and necessary war measure for suppressing said rebellion, do, on this first day of January, in the year of our Lord one thousand eight hundred and sixty-three, and in accordance with my purpose so to do publicly proclaimed for the full period of one hundred days, from the day first above mentioned, order and designate as the states and parts of states wherein the people thereof, respectively, are this day in rebellion against the United States, the following, to wit: . . .

[B]y virtue of the power, and for the purpose aforesaid, I do order and declare that all persons held as slaves within said designated states, and parts of states are and henceforward shall be free, and that the executive government of the United States, including the military and naval authorities thereof, will recognize and maintain the freedom of said persons.

And I hereby enjoin upon the people so declared to be free to abstain from all violence, unless in necessary self-defense, and I recommend to them that, in all cases when allowed, they labor faithfully for reasonable wages.

And I further declare and make known that such persons of suitable condition will be received into the armed service of the United States to garrison forts, positions, stations, and other places, and to man vessels of all sorts in said service.

And upon this act, sincerely believed to be an act of justice, warranted by the Constitution upon military necessity, I invoke the considerate judgment of mankind and the gracious favor of Almighty God.

In witness whereof, I have hereunto set my hand and caused the seal of the United States to be affixed.

Done at the City of Washington, this first day of January, in the year of our Lord one thousand eight hundred and sixty-three, and of the independence of the United States of America the eighty-seventh.

[L.S.]

By the President: ABRAHAM LINCOLN

WILLIAM H. SEWARD, Secretary of State.

20

Letter to Erastus Corning and Others

June 12, 1863

In this letter Lincoln responds to harsh criticism by New York merchant and railroad financier Corning and others regarding the suspension of habeas corpus and perceived abridgments of civil rights. Lincoln's defense is the Constitution. Appealing to their common and ultimate goal of preserving the union, Lincoln disagrees only about the means of doing so. He calls upon them to forgo partisanship, to designate themselves as "American citizens" rather than as "Democrats," but he specifies many well-known Democrats including Andrew Jackson (whom Lincoln knew Corning had supported) who had upheld the suspension of habeas corpus in less dire circumstances. He also points out that others might fault him for not applying military measures sooner and more strictly. Corning was not persuaded and responded by condemning Lincoln's "pretensions to more than regal authority."

[UNABRIDGED]
Executive Mansion, Washington
Hon. Erastus Corning & others

Gentlemen

Your letter of May 19th enclosing the resolutions of a public meeting held at Albany, N.Y., on the 16th of the same month was received several days ago.

The resolutions, as I understand them, are resolvable into

two propositions—first, the expression of a purpose to sustain the cause of the union, to secure peace through victory, and to support the administration in every constitutional and lawful measure to suppress the rebellion; and secondly, a declaration of censure upon the administration for supposed unconstitutional action such as the making of military arrests.

And from the two propositions a third is deduced, which is that the gentlemen composing the meeting are resolved on doing their part to maintain our common government and country, despite the folly or wickedness as they may conceive of any administration. This position is eminently patriotic, and as such, I thank the meeting and congratulate the nation for it. My own purpose is the same, so that the meeting and myself have a common object, and can have no difference except in the choice of means or measures for effecting that object.

And here I ought to close this paper, and would close it if there were no apprehension that more injurious consequences than any merely personal to myself might follow the censures systematically cast upon me for doing what, in my view of duty, I could not forbear. The resolutions promise to support me in every constitutional and lawful measure to suppress the rebellion, and I have not knowingly employed, nor shall knowingly employ, any other. But the meeting, by their resolutions, assert and argue that certain military arrests and proceedings following them for which I am ultimately responsible are unconstitutional. I think they are not. The resolutions quote from the Constitution the definition of treason, and also the limiting safeguards and guarantees therein provided for the citizen on trials for treason and on his being held to answer for capital or otherwise infamous crimes, and, in criminal prosecutions, his right to a speedy and public trial by an impartial jury. They proceed to resolve "that these safeguards of the rights of the citizen against the pretensions of arbitrary power were intended more *especially* for his protection in times of civil commotion." And, apparently, to demonstrate the proposition, the resolutions proceed, "They were secured substantially to the English people *after* years of protracted civil war and were adopted into our Constitution at the *close* of the revolution." Would not the demonstration have been better if it could have been truly said that these safeguards had been adopted and applied *during* the civil wars and *during* our revolution, instead of *after* the one and at the *close* of the other. I too am devotedly for them *after* civil war, and *before* civil war, and at all times "except when, in cases of rebellion or invasion, the public safety may require" their suspension. The resolutions proceed to tell us that these safeguards "have stood the test of seventy-six years of trial under our republican system, under circumstances which show that while they constitute the foundation of all free government, they are the elements of the enduring stability of the republic." No one denies that they have so stood the test up to the beginning of the present rebellion if we except a certain matter at New Orleans hereafter to be mentioned, nor does anyone question that they will stand the same test much longer after the rebellion closes. But these provisions of the Constitution have no application to the case we have in hand, because the arrests complained of were not made for treason—that is, not for *the* treason defined in the Constitution and upon the conviction of which the punishment is death—nor yet were they made to hold persons to answer for any capital or otherwise infamous crimes; nor were the proceedings following, in any constitutional or legal sense, "criminal prosecutions." The arrests were made on totally different grounds, and the proceedings following accorded with the grounds of the arrests. Let us consider the real case with which we are dealing and apply to it the parts of the Constitution plainly made for such cases.

Prior to my installation here it had been inculcated that any state had a lawful right to secede from the national union, and that it would be expedient to exercise the right whenever the devotees of the doctrine should fail to elect a president to their own liking. I was elected contrary to their liking and, accordingly, so far as it was legally possible, they had taken seven states out of the union, had seized many of the United States' forts, and had fired upon the United States flag all before I was inaugurated and, of course, before I had done any official act whatever. The rebellion thus began soon ran into the present Civil War, and in certain respects it began on very unequal terms between the parties. The insurgents had been preparing for it more than thirty years, while the government had taken no steps to resist them. The former had carefully considered all the means which could be turned to their account. It undoubtedly was a well-pondered reliance with them that in their own unrestricted effort to destroy union, Constitution, and law, all together, the government would in great degree be restrained by the same Constitution and law from arresting their progress. Their sympathizers pervaded all departments of the government and nearly all communities of the people. From this material, under cover of "liberty of speech," "liberty of the press," and "habeas corpus," they hoped to keep on foot amongst us a most efficient corps of spies, informers, suppliers, and aiders and abettors of their cause in a thousand ways. They knew that in times such as they were inaugurating, by the Constitution itself the "habeas corpus" might be suspended, but they also knew they had friends who would make a question as to *who* was to suspend it; meanwhile their spies and others might remain at large to help on their cause. Or if, as has happened, the executive should suspend the writ without ruinous waste of time, instances of arresting innocent persons might occur, as are always likely to occur in such cases. And then a clamor could be raised in regard to this, which might be, at least, of some service to the insurgent cause. It needed no very keen perception to discover this part of the enemies' program so soon, as by open hostilities their machinery was fairly put in motion. Yet, thoroughly imbued with a reverence for the guaranteed rights of individuals, I was slow to adopt the strong measures, which by degrees I have been forced to regard as being within the exceptions of the Constitution and as indispensable to the public safety. Nothing is better known to history than that courts of justice are utterly incompetent to such cases. Civil courts are organized chiefly for trials of individuals or, at most, a few individuals acting in concert, and this in quiet times and on charges of crimes well defined in the law. Even in times of peace, bands of horse thieves and robbers frequently grow too numerous and powerful for the ordinary courts of justice. But what comparison, in numbers, have such bands ever borne to the insurgent sympathizers even in many of the loyal states? Again, a jury too frequently have at least one member more ready to hang the panel than to hang the traitor. And yet again, he who dissuades one man from volunteering, or induces one soldier to desert, weakens the Union cause as much as he who kills a Union soldier in battle. Yet this dissuasion, or inducement, may be so conducted as to be no defined crime of which any civil court would take cognizance.

Ours is a case of rebellion—so-called by the resolutions

before me—in fact, a clear, flagrant, and gigantic case of rebellion, and the provision of the Constitution that "The privilege of the writ of habeas corpus shall not be suspended, unless when, in cases of rebellion or invasion, the public safety may require it" is *the* provision which specially applies to our present case. This provision plainly attests the understanding of those who made the Constitution that ordinary courts of justice are inadequate to "cases of rebellion"—attests their purpose that in such cases, men may be held in custody whom the courts, acting on ordinary rules, would discharge. Habeas corpus does not discharge men who are proved to be guilty of defined crime, and its suspension is allowed by the Constitution on purpose that men may be arrested and held who cannot be proved to be guilty of defined crime "when, in cases of rebellion or invasion, the public safety may require it." This is precisely our present case—a case of rebellion, wherein the public safety does require the suspension. Indeed, arrests by process of courts, and arrests in cases of rebellion, do not proceed altogether upon the same basis. The former is directed at the small percentage of ordinary and continuous perpetration of crime, while the latter is directed at sudden and extensive uprisings against the government which, at most, will succeed or fail in no great length of time. In the latter case, arrests are made not so much for what has been done as for what probably would be done. The latter is more for the preventive and less for the vindictive than the former. In such cases the purposes of men are much more easily understood than in cases of ordinary crime. The man who stands by and says nothing when the peril of his government is discussed cannot be misunderstood. If not hindered, he is sure to help the enemy. Much more, if he talks ambiguously—talks for his country with "buts" and "ifs" and "ands."

Of how little value the constitutional provision I have quoted will be rendered if arrests shall never be made until defined crimes shall have been committed may be illustrated by a few notable examples. Gen. John C. Breckenridge, Gen. Robert E. Lee, Gen. Joseph E. Johnston, Gen. John B. Magruder, Gen. William B. Preston, Gen. Simon B. Buckner, and Commodore [Franklin] Buchanan, now occupying the very highest places in the rebel war service, were all within the power of the government since the rebellion began and were nearly as well known to be traitors then as now. Unquestionably if we had seized and held them, the insurgent cause would be much weaker. But no one of them had then committed any crime defined in the law. Every one of them if arrested would have been discharged on habeas corpus were the writ allowed to operate. In view of these and similar cases, I think the time not unlikely to come when I shall be blamed for having made too few arrests rather than too many.

By the third resolution the meeting indicate their opinion that military arrests may be constitutional in localities where rebellion actually exists, but that such arrests are unconstitutional in localities where rebellion or insurrection does not actually exist. They insist that such arrests shall not be made "outside of the lines of necessary military occupation and the scenes of insurrection." Inasmuch, however, as the Constitution itself makes no such distinction, I am unable to believe that there is any such constitutional distinction. I concede that the class of arrests complained of can be constitutional only when, in cases of rebellion or invasion, the public safety may require them; and I insist that in such cases they are constitutional *wherever* the public safety does require them—as well in places to which they may prevent the rebellion extending, as in those where it may be already prevailing—as well where they may restrain mischievous interference with the raising and supplying of armies to suppress the rebellion, as where the rebellion may actually be—as well where they may restrain the enticing men out of the army, as where they would prevent mutiny in the army—equally constitutional at all places where they will conduce to the public safety, as against the dangers of rebellion or invasion.

Take the particular case mentioned by the meeting. They assert in substance that Mr. Vallandigham was, by a military commander, seized and tried "for no other reason than words addressed to a public meeting in criticism of the course of the administration and in condemnation of the military orders of that general." Now, if there be no mistake about this—if this assertion is the truth and the whole truth—if there was no other reason for the arrest, then I concede that the arrest was wrong. But the arrest, as I understand, was made for a very different reason. Mr. Vallandigham avows his hostility to the war on the part of the Union, and his arrest was made because he was laboring, with some effect, to prevent the raising of troops, to encourage desertions from the army, and to leave the rebellion without an adequate military force to suppress it. He was not arrested because he was damaging the political prospects of the administration, or the personal interests of the commanding general, but because he was damaging the army, upon the existence and vigor of which the life of the nation depends. He was warring upon the military, and this gave the military constitutional jurisdiction to lay hands upon him. If Mr. Vallandigham was not damaging the military power of the country, then his arrest was made on mistake of fact, which I would be glad to correct on reasonably satisfactory evidence.

I understand the meeting, whose resolutions I am considering, to be in favor of suppressing the rebellion by military force—by armies. Long experience has shown that armies cannot be maintained unless desertion shall be punished by the severe penalty of death. The case requires, and the law and the Constitution sanction, this punishment. Must I shoot a simpleminded soldier boy who deserts, while I must not touch a hair of a wily agitator who induces him to desert? This is nonetheless injurious when effected by getting a father, or brother, or friend into a public meeting and there working upon his feeling till he is persuaded to write the soldier boy that he is fighting in a bad cause for a wicked administration of a contemptible government, too weak to arrest and punish him if he shall desert. I think that in such a case, to silence the agitator and save the boy is not only constitutional but, withal, a great mercy.

If I be wrong on this question of constitutional power, my error lies in believing that certain proceedings are constitutional when, in cases of rebellion or invasion, the public safety requires them, which would not be constitutional when, in absence of rebellion or invasion, the public safety does not require them—in other words, that the Constitution is not in its application in all respects the same, in cases of rebellion or invasion involving the public safety, as it is in times of profound peace and public security. The Constitution itself makes the distinction, and I can no more be persuaded that the government can constitutionally take no strong measure in time of rebellion, because it can be shown that the same could not be lawfully taken in time of peace, than I can be persuaded that a particular drug is not good medicine for a sick man because it can be shown to not be good food for a well one. Nor am I able to appreciate the danger apprehended by the meeting that the American people will, by means of military arrests during the rebellion, lose the right of public discussion, the liberty of speech and the press, the law of evidence, trial by jury, and habeas corpus throughout the indefinite peaceful future which I trust lies before them, any more than I am able to believe that a man could contract so strong an appetite for emetics during temporary illness as to persist in feeding upon them through the remainder of his healthful life.

In giving the resolutions that earnest consideration which you request of me, I cannot overlook the fact that the meeting speak as "Democrats." Nor can I, with full respect for their known intelligence and the fairly presumed deliberation with which they prepared their resolutions, be permitted to suppose that this occurred by accident or in any way other than that they preferred to designate themselves "Democrats" rather than "American citizens." In this time of national peril I would have preferred to meet you upon a level one step higher than any party platform, because I am sure that from such more elevated position, we could do better battle for the country we all love than we possibly can from those lower ones where, from the force of habit, the prejudices of the past and selfish hopes of the future, we are sure to expend much of our ingenuity and strength in finding fault with and aiming blows at each other. But since you have denied me this, I will yet be thankful, for the country's sake, that not all Democrats have done so. He on whose discretionary judgment Mr. Vallandigham was arrested and tried is a Democrat, having no old party affinity with me, and the judge who rejected the constitutional view expressed in these resolutions, by refusing to discharge Mr. V. on habeas corpus, is a Democrat of better days than these, having received his judicial mantle at the hands of President Jackson. And still more, of all those Democrats who are nobly exposing their lives and shedding their blood on the battlefield, I have learned that many approve the course taken with Mr. V. while I have not heard of a single one condemning it. I cannot assert that there are none such.

And the name of President Jackson recalls a bit of pertinent history. After the battle of New Orleans, and while the fact that the treaty of peace had been concluded was well known in the city but before official knowledge of it had arrived, Gen. Jackson still maintained martial, or military law. Now that it could be said the war was over, the clamor against martial law, which had existed from the first, grew more furious. Among other things, a Mr. Louiallier published a denunciatory newspaper article. Gen. Jackson arrested him. A lawyer by the name of Morel procured the U.S. Judge Hall to order a writ of habeas corpus to release Mr. Louiallier. Gen. Jackson arrested both the lawyer and the judge. A Mr. Hollander ventured to say of some part of the matter that "it was a dirty trick." Gen. Jackson arrested him. When the officer undertook to serve the writ of habeas corpus, Gen. Jackson took it from him and sent him away with a copy. Holding the judge in custody a few days, the general sent him beyond the limits of his encampment and set him at liberty with an order to remain till the ratification of peace should be regularly announced or until the British should have left the southern coast. A day or two more elapsed, the ratification of the treaty of peace was regularly announced, and the judge and others were fully liberated. A few days more, and the judge called Gen. Jackson into court and fined him a thousand dollars for having arrested him and the others named. The general paid the fine, and there the matter rested for nearly thirty years, when Congress refunded principal and interest. The late Senator Douglas, then in the House of Representatives, took a leading part in the debate in which the constitutional question was much discussed. I am not prepared to say whom the journals would show to have voted for the measure.

It may be remarked: First, that we had the same Constitution then as now. Secondly, that we then had a case of invasion, and that now we have a case of rebellion. And Thirdly, that the permanent right of the people to public discussion, the liberty of speech and the press, the trial by jury, the law of evidence, and the habeas corpus suffered no detriment whatever by that conduct of Gen. Jackson or its subsequent approval by the American Congress.

And yet, let me say that in my own discretion, I do not know whether I would have ordered the arrest of Mr. V. While I cannot shift the responsibility from myself, I hold that, as a general rule, the commander in the field is the better judge of the necessity in any particular case. Of course I must practice a general directory and revisory power in the matter.

One of the resolutions expresses the opinion of the meeting that arbitrary arrests will have the effect to divide and distract those who should be united in suppressing the rebellion, and I am specifically called on to discharge Mr. Vallandigham. I regard this as, at least, a fair appeal to me, on the expediency of exercising a constitutional power which I think exists. In response to such appeal I have to say it gave me pain when I learned that Mr. V. had been arrested—that is, I was pained that there should have seemed to be a necessity for arresting him—and that it will afford me great pleasure to discharge him so soon as I can, by any means, believe the public safety will not suffer by it. I further say, that as the war progresses, it appears to me opinion and action, which were in great confusion at first, take shape and fall into more regular channels, so that the necessity for arbitrary dealing with them gradually decreases. I have every reason to desire that it would cease altogether, and far from the least is my regard for the opinions and wishes of those who, like the meeting at Albany, declare their purpose to sustain the government in every constitutional and lawful measure to suppress the rebellion. Still, I must continue to do so much as may seem to be required by the public safety.

A. LINCOLN.

21

"Order of Retaliation"

July 30, 1863

This strong language shows Lincoln's temper. Lincoln is respond-
ing to more than rebellion and treason against the United
States; actions of the Confederates against African American
soldiers were a crime against civilization, "a relapse into barbarism." He declares that the government must protect its citizens and that color is no distinction. Notably, it was issued five
years almost to the day ahead of ratification of the Fourteenth
Amendment granting citizenship to African Americans.

[UNABRIDGED]
Order of Retaliation
Executive Mansion, Washington, D.C.

It is the duty of every government to give protection to its citizens of whatever class, color, or condition, and especially to
those who are duly organized as soldiers in the public service.
The law of nations and the usages and customs of war as carried on by civilized powers permit no distinction as to color in
the treatment of prisoners of war as public enemies. To sell or
enslave any captured person on account of his color, and for
no offense against the laws of war, is a relapse into barbarism
and a crime against the civilization of the age.

The government of the United States will give the same
protection to all its soldiers, and if the enemy shall sell or

enslave anyone because of his color, the offense shall be punished by retaliation upon the enemy's prisoners in our possession.

It is therefore ordered that for every soldier of the United States killed in violation of the laws of war, a rebel soldier shall be executed; and for every one enslaved by the enemy or sold into slavery, a rebel soldier shall be placed at hard labor on the public works and continued at such labor until the other shall be released and receive the treatment due to a prisoner of war.

ABRAHAM LINCOLN

22

Letter to Nathaniel P. Banks (Louisiana) on Reconstruction

August 5, 1863

Lincoln's letter to Nathaniel Banks, the Union general in charge of occupied Louisiana, offers a glimpse into his thinking on the postwar South. Because Lincoln was murdered before the war's conclusion, to this day opinions differ on how Lincoln would have reconstructed the defeated Confederacy. For this reason, his plan for Louisiana looms large. Lincoln expresses hope that emancipation will be extended, but he is adamant that the Emancipation Proclamation must never be "retracted." He advocates education of former slaves and recommends that Louisiana create a new and better system of race relations. In answer to why former Confederates would agree to such a change, he reminds Banks that those men would not want to perpetuate a "recurrence" of a war they are losing.

[ABRIDGED]
Executive Mansion, Washington
To Nathaniel P. Banks

My dear General Banks

. . . While I very well know what I would be glad for Louisiana to do, it is quite a different thing for me to assume direction of the matter. I would be glad for her to make a new constitution recognizing the Emancipation Proclamation and adopting emancipation in those parts of the state to which the proclamation does not apply. And while she is at it, I think it would not be objectionable for her to adopt some practical system by which the two races could gradually live themselves out of their old relation to each other and both come out better prepared for the new. Education for young blacks should be included in the plan. After all, the power, or element, of "contract" may be sufficient for this probationary period and by its simplicity and flexibility may be the better.

As an antislavery man I have a motive to desire emancipation which proslavery men do not have, but even they have strong enough reason to thus place themselves again under the shield of the union and to thus perpetually hedge against the recurrence of the scenes through which we are now passing.

Gov. Shepley has informed me that Mr. Durant is now taking a registry, with a view to the election of a constitutional convention in Louisiana. This, to me, appears proper. If such convention were to ask my views, I could present little else than what I now say to you. I think the thing should be pushed forward so that, if possible, its mature work may reach here by the meeting of Congress.

For my own part I think I shall not, in any event, retract the Emancipation Proclamation, nor, as executive, ever return to slavery any person who is free by the terms of that proclamation or by any of the acts of Congress.

If Louisiana shall send members to Congress, their admission to seats will depend, as you know, upon the respective houses and not upon the president.

If these views can be of any advantage in giving shape and impetus to action there, I shall be glad for you to use them prudently for that object. Of course you will confer with intelligent and trusty citizens of the state, among whom I would suggest Messrs. Flanders, Hahn, and Durant, and to each of whom I now think I may send copies of this letter. Still, it is perhaps better to not make the letter generally public. Yours very truly

A. LINCOLN

Letter to James C. Conkling on Emancipation

August 26, 1863

James Conkling, an oldtime friend and supporter of Abraham Lincoln, requested Lincoln speak at a mass meeting in Springfield scheduled for September 1863. Lincoln could not attend, but he wanted to use the opportunity to speak to "unconditional union men" about a policy many opposed—emancipation. With logic reminiscent of his earlier letter to Horace Greeley, Lincoln writes about the need to defend the union. Within that larger picture Lincoln eloquently defends the importance of freedom and of judging men by their actions rather than the color of their skin. The letter was accompanied by a brief, private note to "My dear Conkling" that read, ". . . You are one of the best public readers. I have but one suggestion. Read it very slowly. And now God bless you, and all good union men."

[UNABRIDGED]
Executive Mansion, Washington
Hon. James C. Conkling

My Dear Sir.

Your letter inviting me to attend a mass meeting of unconditional union men, to be held at the capital of Illinois, on the 3d day of September, has been received.

It would be very agreeable to me to thus meet my old

friends at my own home, but I cannot, just now, be absent from here so long as a visit there would require.

The meeting is to be of all those who maintain unconditional devotion to the union, and I am sure my old political friends will thank me for tendering, as I do, the nation's gratitude to those other noble men whom no partisan malice or partisan hope can make false to the nation's life.

There are those who are dissatisfied with me. To such I would say: You desire peace, and you blame me that we do not have it. But how can we attain it? There are but three conceivable ways. First, to suppress the rebellion by force of arms. This, I am trying to do. Are you for it? If you are, so far we are agreed. If you are not for it, a second way is to give up the union. I am against this.

Are you for it? If you are, you should say so plainly. If you are not for force, nor yet for dissolution, there only remains some imaginable compromise. I do not believe any compromise embracing the maintenance of the union is now possible. All I learn leads to a directly opposite belief. The strength of the rebellion is its military—its army. That army dominates all the country and all the people within its range. Any offer of terms made by any man or men within that range in opposition to that army is simply nothing for the present, because such man or men have no power whatever to enforce their side of a compromise, if one were made with them. To illustrate—suppose refugees from the South, and peace men of the North, get together in convention and frame and proclaim a compromise embracing a restoration of the union. In what way can that compromise be used to keep Lee's army out of Pennsylvania? Meade's army can keep Lee's army out of Pennsylvania and, I think, can ultimately drive it out of existence. But no paper compromise, to which the controllers of

Lee's army are not agreed, can at all affect that army. In an effort at such compromise we should waste time, which the enemy would improve to our disadvantage, and that would be all. A compromise, to be effective, must be made either with those who control the rebel army or with the people first liberated from the domination of that army by the success of our own army. Now allow me to assure you that no word or intimation from that rebel army, or from any of the men controlling it, in relation to any peace compromise has ever come to my knowledge or belief. All charges and insinuations to the contrary are deceptive and groundless. And I promise you that if any such proposition shall hereafter come, it shall not be rejected and kept a secret from you. I freely acknowledge myself the servant of the people, according to the bond of service—the United States Constitution—and that, as such, I am responsible to them.

But, to be plain, you are dissatisfied with me about the Negro. Quite likely there is a difference of opinion between you and myself upon that subject. I certainly wish that all men could be free, while I suppose you do not. Yet I have neither adopted nor proposed any measure which is not consistent with even your view, provided you are for the union. I suggested compensated emancipation, to which you replied you wished not to be taxed to buy Negroes. But I had not asked you to be taxed to buy Negroes, except in such way as to save you from greater taxation to save the union exclusively by other means.

You dislike the Emancipation Proclamation and, perhaps, would have it retracted. You say it is unconstitutional—I think differently. I think the Constitution invests its commander in chief with the law of war in time of war. The most that can be said, if so much, is that slaves are property. Is there—has there ever been—any question that by the law of war, property, both of enemies and friends, may be taken when needed? And is it not needed whenever taking it helps us or hurts the enemy? Armies the world over destroy enemies' property when they cannot use it, and even destroy their own to keep it from the enemy. Civilized belligerents do all in their power to help themselves or hurt the enemy except a few things regarded as barbarous or cruel. Among the exceptions are the massacre of vanquished foes and noncombatants, male and female.

But the proclamation, as law, either is valid or is not valid. If it is not valid, it needs no retraction. If it is valid, it cannot be retracted any more than the dead can be brought to life. Some of you profess to think its retraction would operate favorably for the union. Why better after the retraction than before the issue? There was more than a year and a half of trial to suppress the rebellion before the proclamation issued, the last one hundred days of which passed under an explicit notice that it was coming unless averted by those in revolt returning to their allegiance. The war has certainly progressed as favorably for us since the issue of the proclamation as before. I know as fully as one can know the opinions of others, that some of the commanders of our armies in the field who have given us our most important successes believe the emancipation policy and the use of colored troops constitute the heaviest blow yet dealt to the rebellion, and that at least one of those important successes could not have been achieved when it was but for the aid of black soldiers. Among the commanders holding these views are some who have never had any affinity with what is called abolitionism, or with Republican Party politics, but who hold them purely as military opinions. I submit these opinions as being entitled to some weight against the objections, often urged, that emancipation and arming the blacks are unwise as military measures and were not adopted, as such, in good faith.

You say you will not fight to free Negroes. Some of them seem willing to fight for you, but no matter. Fight you, then, exclusively to save the union. I issued the proclamation on purpose to aid you in saving the union. Whenever you shall have conquered all resistance to the union, if I shall urge you to continue fighting, it will be an apt time, then, for you to declare you will not fight to free Negroes.

I thought that in your struggle for the union, to whatever extent the Negroes should cease helping the enemy, to that extent it weakened the enemy in his resistance to you. Do you think differently? I thought that whatever Negroes can be got to do as soldiers leaves just so much less for white soldiers to do in saving the union. Does it appear otherwise to you? But Negroes, like other people, act upon motives. Why should they do anything for us if we will do nothing for them? If they stake their lives for us, they must be prompted by the strongest motive—even the promise of freedom. And the promise being made, must be kept.

The signs look better. The Father of Waters again goes unvexed to the sea. Thanks to the great Northwest for it. Nor yet wholly to them. Three hundred miles up, they met New England, Empire, Keystone, and Jersey hewing their way right and left. The sunny South too, in more colors than one, also lent a hand. On the spot, their part of the history was jotted down in black and white. The job was a great national one, and let none be banned who bore an honorable part in it. And while those who have cleared the great river may well be proud, even that is not all. It is hard to say that anything has been more bravely and well done than at Antietam, Murfreesboro, Gettysburg, and on many fields of lesser note. Nor must

Uncle Sam's web feet be forgotten. At all the watery margins they have been present. Not only on the deep sea, the broad bay, and the rapid river, but also up the narrow muddy bayou and wherever the ground was a little damp they have been and made their tracks. Thanks to all. For the great republic—for the principle it lives by and keeps alive—for man's vast future—thanks to all.

Peace does not appear so distant as it did. I hope it will come soon, and come to stay, and so come as to be worth the keeping in all future time. It will then have been proved that, among free men, there can be no successful appeal from the ballot to the bullet, and that they who take such appeal are sure to lose their case and pay the cost. And then, there will be some black men who can remember that with silent tongue, and clenched teeth, and steady eye, and well-poised bayonet, they have helped mankind on to this great consummation, while, I fear, there will be some white ones unable to forget that, with malignant heart and deceitful speech, they have strove to hinder it.

Still let us not be oversanguine of a speedy final triumph. Let us be quite sober. Let us diligently apply the means, never doubting that a just God, in His own good time, will give us the rightful result. Yours very truly

A. LINCOLN.

24

Gettysburg Address

November 19, 1863

The twenty-thousand-strong crowd had come to hear Edward Everett speak of valor and values and victory. None anticipated the president's confession, the benediction, and the challenge he set forth in the sweep of a few sentences. With the Gettysburg Address, Lincoln proclaims the hopeful determination of the human spirit for freedom.

Lincoln speaks a language of love, patriotism, and piety. Human liberty and democracy were at stake in this war. What would victory in this awful war look like? Lincoln's vision was at once conservative and revolutionary. More than simply preserving the liberty of the fathers, the new nation, "under God," would have "a new birth of freedom."

[UNABRIDGED]
*Address delivered at the dedication
of the cemetery at Gettysburg*

Four score and seven years ago our fathers brought forth on this continent a new nation, conceived in liberty and dedicated to the proposition that all men are created equal.

Now we are engaged in a great civil war, testing whether that nation, or any nation so conceived and so dedicated, can long endure. We are met on a great battlefield of that war. We have come to dedicate a portion of that field as a final resting place for those who here gave their lives that that nation might live. It is altogether fitting and proper that we should do this.

But, in a larger sense, we cannot dedicate—we cannot consecrate—we cannot hallow—this ground. The brave men, living and dead, who struggled here have consecrated it far above our poor power to add or detract. The world will little note nor long remember what we say here, but it can never forget what they did here. It is for us the living, rather, to be dedicated here to the unfinished work which they who fought here have thus far so nobly advanced. It is rather for us to be here dedicated to the great task remaining before us—that from these honored dead we take increased devotion to that cause for which they gave the last full measure of devotion— that we here highly resolve that these dead shall not have died in vain—that this nation, under God, shall have a new birth of freedom—and that government of the people, by the people, for the people shall not perish from the earth.

ABRAHAM LINCOLN.

25

Annual Message to Congress

December 8, 1863

Lincoln's annual message in 1863 was more optimistic than his previous messages. As usual, the majority of the report was routine, written by his advisers and cabinet members. This excerpt, written in Lincoln's hand, is significant because it shows his summary of the progress made on emancipation, almost one year since its passage. While a year earlier, when he first announced his plans, "hope, and fear, and doubt contended in uncertain conflict," Lincoln now announces that the proclamation has proved a vivid success. True to himself and his ideals, Lincoln asserts that rescinding the freedom extended African Americans, as some suggested Lincoln do to procure an immediate peace, would be "a cruel and an astounding breach of faith."

[ABRIDGED]

Fellow citizens of the Senate and House of Representatives:

... When Congress assembled a year ago the war had already lasted nearly twenty months, and there had been many conflicts on both land and sea, with varying results.

The rebellion had been pressed back into reduced limits, yet the tone of public feeling and opinion, at home and abroad, was not satisfactory. With other signs, the popular elections, then just past, indicated uneasiness among ourselves, while amid much that was cold and menacing the kindest words coming from Europe were uttered in accents of pity that we were too blind to surrender a hopeless cause. Our commerce was suffering greatly by a few armed vessels built upon and furnished from foreign shores, and we were threatened with such additions from the same quarter as would sweep our trade from the sea and raise our blockade. We had failed to elicit from European governments anything hopeful upon this subject. The preliminary emancipation proclamation, issued in September, was running its assigned period to the beginning of the new year. A month later the final proclamation came, including the announcement that colored men of suitable condition would be received into the war service. The policy of emancipation, and of employing black soldiers, gave to the future a new aspect about which hope, and fear, and doubt contended in uncertain conflict. According to our political system, as a matter of civil administration, the general government had no lawful power to effect emancipation in any state, and for a long time it had been hoped that the rebellion could be suppressed without resorting to it as a military measure. It was all the while deemed possible that the necessity for it might come, and that if it should, the crisis of the contest would then be presented. It came and, as was anticipated, it was followed by dark and doubtful days. Eleven months having now passed, we are permitted to take another review. The rebel borders are pressed still further back, and by the complete opening of the Mississippi the country dominated by the rebellion is divided into distinct parts, with no practical communication between them. Tennessee and Arkansas have been substantially cleared of insurgent control, and influential citizens in each, owners of slaves and advocates of slavery at the beginning of the rebellion, now declare openly for emancipation in their respective states. Of those states not included in the Emancipation Proclamation, Maryland and Missouri, neither of which three years ago would tolerate any restraint upon the extension of slavery into new territories, only dispute now as to the best mode of removing it within their own limits.

Of those who were slaves at the beginning of the rebellion, full one hundred thousand are now in the United States military service, about one-half of which number actually bear arms in the ranks, thus giving the double advantage of taking so much labor from the insurgent cause and supplying the places which otherwise must be filled with so many white men. So far as tested, it is difficult to say they are not as good soldiers as any. No servile insurrection or tendency to violence or cruelty has marked the measures of emancipation and arming the blacks. These measures have been much discussed in foreign countries, and contemporary with such discussion the tone of public sentiment there is much improved. At home the same measures have been fully discussed, supported, criticized, and denounced, and the annual elections following are highly encouraging to those whose official duty it is to bear the country through this great trial. Thus we have the new reckoning. The crisis which threatened to divide the friends of the union is past.

Looking now to the present and future, and with reference to a resumption of the national authority within the states wherein that authority has been suspended, I have thought fit to issue a proclamation, a copy of which is herewith transmitted. On examination of this proclamation it will appear, as is believed, that nothing is attempted beyond what is amply justified by the Constitution. True, the form of an oath is given, but no man is coerced to take it. The man is only promised a pardon in case he voluntarily takes the oath.

The Constitution authorizes the executive to grant or withhold the pardon at his own absolute discretion, and this includes the power to grant on terms as is fully established by judicial and other authorities.

It is also proffered that if, in any of the states named, a state government shall be, in the mode prescribed, set up, such government shall be recognized and guaranteed by the United States, and that under it the state shall, on the constitutional conditions, be protected against invasion and domestic violence. The constitutional obligation of the United States to guarantee to every state in the union a republican form of government, and to protect the state in the cases stated, is explicit and full. But why tender the benefits of this provision only to a state government set up in this particular way? This section of the Constitution contemplates a case wherein the element within a state favorable to republican government, in the union, may be too feeble for an opposite and hostile element external to or even within the state, and such are precisely the cases with which we are now dealing.

An attempt to guarantee and protect a revived state government, constructed in whole or in preponderating part from the very element against whose hostility and violence it is to be protected, is simply absurd. There must be a test by which to separate the opposing elements so as to build only from the sound, and that test is a sufficiently liberal one, which accepts as sound whoever will make a sworn recantation of his former unsoundness.

But if it be proper to require, as a test of admission to the political body, an oath of allegiance to the Constitution of the United States, and to the union under it, why also to the laws and proclamations in regard to slavery? Those laws and proclamations were enacted and put forth for the purpose of aiding in the suppression of the rebellion. To give them their fullest effect, there had to be a pledge for their maintenance. In my judgment they have aided, and will further aid, the cause for which they were intended. To now abandon them would be not only to relinquish a lever of power but would also be a cruel and an astounding breach of faith. I may add at this point, that while I remain in my present position I shall not attempt to retract or modify the Emancipation Proclamation, nor shall I return to slavery any person who is free by the terms of that proclamation or by any of the acts of Congress. For these and other reasons it is thought best that support of these measures shall be included in the oath, and it is believed the executive may lawfully claim it in return for pardon and restoration of forfeited rights, which he has clear constitutional power to withhold altogether or grant upon the terms which he shall deem wisest for the public interest. It should be observed, also, that this part of the oath is subject to the modifying and abrogating power of legislation and supreme judicial decision.

The proposed acquiescence of the national executive in any reasonable temporary state arrangement for the freed people is made with the view of possibly modifying the confusion and destitution which must, at best, attend all classes by a total revolution of labor throughout whole states. It is hoped that the already deeply afflicted people in those states may be somewhat more ready to give up the cause of their affliction if, to this extent, this vital matter be left to themselves, while no power of the national executive to prevent an abuse is abridged by the proposition.

The suggestion in the proclamation as to maintaining the

political framework of the states on what is called reconstruction is made in the hope that it may do good without danger of harm. It will save labor and avoid great confusion.

But why any proclamation now upon this subject? This question is beset with the conflicting views that the step might be delayed too long or be taken too soon. In some states the elements for resumption seem ready for action but remain inactive, apparently for want of a rallying point—a plan of action. Why shall A adopt the plan of B, rather than B that of A? And if A and B should agree, how can they know but that the general government here will reject their plan? By the proclamation a plan is presented which may be accepted by them as a rallying point and which they are assured in advance will not be rejected here. This may bring them to act sooner than they otherwise would.

The objections to a premature presentation of a plan by the national executive consists in the danger of committals on points which could be more safely left to further developments. Care has been taken to so shape the document as to avoid embarrassments from this source. Saying that on certain terms certain classes will be pardoned, with rights restored, it is not said that other classes or other terms will never be included. Saying that reconstruction will be accepted if presented in a specified way, it is not said it will never be accepted in any other way.

The movements by state action for emancipation in several of the states not included in the Emancipation Proclamation are matters of profound gratulation. And while I do not repeat in detail what I have heretofore so earnestly urged upon this subject, my general views and feelings remain unchanged, and I trust that Congress will omit no fair opportunity of aiding these important steps to a great consummation.

In the midst of other cares, however important, we must not lose sight of the fact that the war power is still our main reliance. To that power alone can we look, yet for a time, to give confidence to the people in the contested regions that the insurgent power will not again overrun them. Until that confidence shall be established, little can be done anywhere for what is called reconstruction. Hence our chiefest care must still be directed to the army and navy, who have thus far borne their harder part so nobly and well. And it may be esteemed fortunate that in giving the greatest efficiency to these indispensable arms, we do also honorably recognize the gallant men, from commander to sentinel, who compose them, and to whom, more than to others, the world must stand indebted for the home of freedom disenthralled, regenerated, enlarged, and perpetuated.

ABRAHAM LINCOLN
Washington

26

Letter to Michael Hahn

March 13, 1864

A resident of Louisiana, Hahn had opposed secession and worked with the federal government in the occupation of New Orleans. He was elected governor of Louisiana in February 1864. In this letter, Lincoln suggests for Hahn's consideration, but not for public knowledge, that some African Americans should have the right to vote. Lincoln's prediction here, that it would be the African American community that would maintain the "jewel of liberty within the family of freedom," would sadly take more than one hundred years to be realized.

[UNABRIDGED]
Private Executive Mansion, Washington
Hon. Michael Hahn

My dear Sir:

I congratulate you on having fixed your name in history as the first Free State governor of Louisiana. Now you are about to have a convention which, among other things, will probably define the elective franchise. I barely suggest for your private consideration whether some of the colored people may not be let in—as, for instance, the very intelligent, and especially those who have fought gallantly in our ranks. They would probably help, in some trying time to come, to keep the jewel of liberty within the family of freedom. But this is only a suggestion, not to the public, but to you alone. Yours truly

A. LINCOLN

27

Address at Sanitary Fair,
Baltimore, Maryland

April 18, 1864

Although initially reluctant to authorize the Sanitary Commission, by 1864 Lincoln valued the organization and the mostly women volunteers' hard work and efficiency in providing Union soldiers with bandages, food, clothing, medicine, and good, clean hospitals. At this Sanitary Fair, one of many fund-raising bazaars to support the work of the commission, Lincoln remarks on the surprising changes wrought by the war, again mentioning God's mysteries. The speech is best known for Lincoln's discussion of the varying, and even opposite, meanings of the word "liberty." Lincoln rejects outright the claim that slavery must have equal rights with liberty. Lincoln is leading the country toward a different definition of liberty—away from the idea that liberty was freedom from government and toward the idea that freedom needed government enforcement.

[UNABRIDGED]
Address at Sanitary Fair, Baltimore, Maryland
Ladies and Gentlemen—Calling to mind that we are in Baltimore, we cannot fail to note that the world moves. Looking upon these many people assembled here to serve, as they best may, the soldiers of the Union, it occurs at once that three years ago, the same soldiers could not so much as pass through Baltimore. The change from then till now is both great and

gratifying. Blessings on the brave men who have wrought the change and the fair women who strive to reward them for it.

But Baltimore suggests more than could happen within Baltimore. The change within Baltimore is part only of a far wider change. When the war began three years ago, neither party nor any man expected it would last till now. Each looked for the end, in some way, long ere today. Neither did any anticipate that domestic slavery would be much affected by the war. But here we are: The war has not ended, and slavery has been much affected—how much needs not now to be recounted. So true is it that man proposes and God disposes.

But we can see the past, though we may not claim to have directed it; and seeing it, in this case, we feel more hopeful and confident for the future.

The world has never had a good definition of the word liberty, and the American people just now are much in want of one. We all declare for liberty, but in using the same word we do not all mean the same thing. With some the word liberty may mean for each man to do as he pleases with himself and the product of his labor; while with others the same word may mean for some men to do as they please with other men and the product of other men's labor. Here are two not only different but incompatible things called by the same name—liberty. And it follows that each of the things is, by the respective parties, called by two different and incompatible names—liberty and tyranny.

The shepherd drives the wolf from the sheep's throat, for which the sheep thanks the shepherd as a liberator, while the wolf denounces him for the same act as the destroyer of liberty, especially as the sheep was a black one. Plainly the sheep and the wolf are not agreed upon a definition of the word liberty, and precisely the same difference prevails today among us human creatures, even in the North, and all professing to love liberty. Hence we behold the processes by which thousands are daily passing from under the yoke of bondage, hailed by some as the advance of liberty and bewailed by others as the destruction of all liberty. Recently, as it seems, the people of Maryland have been doing something to define liberty, and thanks to them that in what they have done, the wolf's dictionary has been repudiated.

It is not very becoming for one in my position to make speeches at great length, but there is another subject upon which I feel that I ought to say a word. A painful rumor—true, I fear—has reached us of the massacre by the rebel forces at Fort Pillow in the west end of Tennessee on the Mississippi River of some three hundred colored soldiers and white officers who had just been overpowered by their assailants. There seems to be some anxiety in the public mind whether the government is doing its duty to the colored soldier and to the service at this point. At the beginning of the war, and for some time, the use of colored troops was not contemplated, and how the change of purpose was wrought I will not now take time to explain. Upon a clear conviction of duty I resolved to turn that element of strength to account, and I am responsible for it to the American people, to the Christian world, to history, and on my final account to God. Having determined to use the Negro as a soldier, there is no way but to give him all the protection given to any other soldier. The difficulty is not in stating the principle but in practically applying it. It is a mistake to suppose the government is indifferent to this matter or is not doing the best it can in regard to it. We do not today know that a colored soldier, or white officer commanding colored soldiers, has been massacred by the rebels when made a prisoner. We fear it, believe it, I may say, but we do not know it. To take the life of one of their prisoners on the assumption that they murder ours, when it is short of certainty that they do murder ours, might be too serious, too cruel a mistake. We are having the Fort Pillow affair thoroughly investigated, and such investigation will probably show conclusively how the truth is. If, after all that has been said, it shall turn out that there has been no massacre at Fort Pillow, it will be almost safe to say there has been none and will be none elsewhere. If there has been the massacre of three hundred there, or even the tenth part of three hundred, it will be conclusively proved, and being so proved, the retribution shall as surely come. It will be [a] matter of grave consideration in what exact course to apply the retribution, but in the supposed case, it must come.

28

Second Inaugural Address

March 4, 1865

Lincoln's second inaugural address, widely regarded as his best speech, is a national prayer of confession. Lincoln's religious feelings deepened during his first term as president, and he came to see God's hand in human events. Yet there remains the sense of him as standing with the hopeless sinners, not the smugly saved. While Lincoln heard both Northern and Southern assertions that God is on their side and while he is willing to admit that he simply does not understand Divine Providence, he asserts nevertheless that Almighty God has His own purposes. Lincoln assigns the South blame for resorting to war, but he is not charging guilt to the South alone. He acknowledges that "American slavery" is a national sin and that God gave the punishment of war "to both North and South." Lincoln's call for malice toward none and charity toward all would go unheeded.

[UNABRIDGED]

Fellow Countrymen:

At this second appearing to take the oath of the presidential office, there is less occasion for an extended address than there was at the first. Then a statement, somewhat in detail, of a course to be pursued seemed fitting and proper. Now, at the expiration of four years, during which public declarations have been constantly called forth on every point and phase of the great contest which still absorbs the attention and engrosses the energies of the nation, little that is new could be presented. The progress of our arms, upon which all else chiefly depends, is as well known to the public as to myself, and it is, I trust, reasonably satisfactory and encouraging to all. With high hope for the future, no prediction in regard to it is ventured.

On the occasion corresponding to this four years ago, all thoughts were anxiously directed to an impending civil war. All dreaded it—all sought to avert it. While the inaugural address was being delivered from this place, devoted altogether to saving the union without war, insurgent agents were in the city seeking to destroy it without war—seeking to dissolve the union and divide effects by negotiation. Both parties deprecated war, but one of them would make war rather than let the nation survive, and the other would accept war rather than let it perish. And the war came.

One-eighth of the whole population were colored slaves, not distributed generally over the union but localized in the Southern part of it. These slaves constituted a peculiar and powerful interest. All knew that this interest was, somehow, the cause of the war. To strengthen, perpetuate, and extend this interest was the object for which the insurgents would rend the union, even by war, while the government claimed no right to do more than to restrict the territorial enlargement of it. Neither party expected for the war the magnitude or the duration which it has already attained. Neither anticipated that the cause of the conflict might cease with, or even before, the conflict itself should cease. Each looked for an easier triumph and a result less fundamental and astounding. Both read the same Bible and pray to the same God, and each invokes His aid against the other. It may seem strange that any men should dare to ask a just God's assistance in wringing their bread from the sweat of other men's faces, but let us judge not that we be not judged. The prayers of both could not be answered; that of neither has been answered fully. The Almighty has His own purposes. "Woe unto the world because of offenses! for it must needs be that offenses come; but woe to that man by whom the offense cometh!" If we shall suppose that American slavery is one of those offenses which, in the providence of God, must needs come, but which, having continued through His appointed time, He now wills to remove, and that He gives to both North and South this terrible war, as the woe due to those by whom the offense came, shall we discern therein any departure from those divine attributes which the believers in a Living God always ascribe to Him? Fondly do we hope—fervently do we pray—that this mighty scourge of war may speedily pass away. Yet, if God wills that it continue until all the wealth piled by the bondman's two hundred and fifty years of unrequited toil shall be sunk and until every drop of blood drawn with the lash shall be paid by another drawn with the sword, as was said three thousand years ago, so still it must be said "the judgments of the Lord are true and righteous altogether."

With malice toward none; with charity for all; with firmness in the right, as God gives us to see the right, let us strive on to finish the work we are in; to bind up the nation's wounds; to care for him who shall have borne the battle, and for his widow, and his orphan—to do all which may achieve and cherish a just and a lasting peace among ourselves and with all nations.

29

Speech from the Balcony, Last Public Address

April 11, 1865

On April 11, just two days after Lee surrendered to Grant, from the White House balcony Lincoln addresses a gathering crowd. Lincoln knows that Reconstruction would not confront one single, unified South but rather "disorganized and discordant elements." Nevertheless, he hopes and expects that a majority of white Southerners would support efforts to reunify the country. Presidential and congressional Reconstruction became fighting points in the years ahead, but here Lincoln discusses the need for cooperation between the executive and the legislative branches of the government. More important, just as Lincoln had done with the Emancipation Proclamation and his answer to Horace Greeley's plea of twenty million, he once again prepares the nation to accept African American citizenship. Lincoln concludes this speech by telling the gathered crowd to expect a further announcement.

[UNABRIDGED]

We meet this evening not in sorrow but in gladness of heart. The evacuation of Petersburg and Richmond, and the surrender of the principal insurgent army give hope of a righteous and speedy peace whose joyous expression cannot be restrained. In the midst of this, however, He, from Whom all blessings flow, must not be forgotten. A call for a national thanksgiving is being prepared and will be duly promulgated.

Nor must those whose harder part gives us the cause of rejoicing be overlooked. Their honors must not be parceled out with others. I myself was near the front and had the high pleasure of transmitting much of the good news to you, but no part of the honor, for plan or execution, is mine. To Gen. Grant, his skillful officers, and brave men all belongs. The gallant navy stood ready but was not in reach to take active part.

By these recent successes the reinauguration of the national authority—reconstruction—which has had a large share of thought from the first, is pressed much more closely upon our attention. It is fraught with great difficulty. Unlike the case of a war between independent nations, there is no authorized organ for us to treat with. No one man has authority to give up the rebellion for any other man. We simply must begin with, and mold from, disorganized and discordant elements. Nor is it a small additional embarrassment that we, the loyal people, differ among ourselves as to the mode, manner, and means of reconstruction.

As a general rule, I abstain from reading the reports of attacks upon myself, wishing not to be provoked by that to which I cannot properly offer an answer. In spite of this precaution, however, it comes to my knowledge that I am much censured for some supposed agency in setting up, and seeking to sustain, the new state government of Louisiana. In this I have done just so much as, and no more than, the public knows. In the annual message of Dec. 1863 and accompanying proclamation, I presented a plan of reconstruction (as the phrase goes) which, I promised, if adopted by any state should be acceptable to and sustained by the executive government of the nation. I distinctly stated that this was not the only plan which might possibly be acceptable, and I also distinctly protested that the executive claimed no right to say when, or whether, members should be admitted to seats in Congress from such states. This plan was, in advance, submitted to the then cabinet and distinctly approved by every member of it. One of them suggested that I should then, and in that connection, apply the Emancipation Proclamation to the theretofore excepted parts of Virginia and Louisiana, that I should drop the suggestion about apprenticeship for freed people, and that I should omit the protest against my own power in regard to the admission of members to Congress. But even he approved every part and parcel of the plan which has since been employed or touched by the action of Louisiana. The new constitution of Louisiana, declaring emancipation for the whole state, practically applies the proclamation to the part previously excepted. It does not adopt apprenticeship for freed people, and it is silent, as it could not well be otherwise, about the admission of members to Congress. So that, as it applies to Louisiana, every member of the cabinet fully approved the plan. The message went to Congress, and I received many commendations of the plan, written and verbal, and not a single objection to it from any professed emancipationist came to my knowledge until after the news reached Washington that the people of Louisiana had begun to move in accordance with it. From about July 1862, I had corresponded with different persons, supposed to be interested, seeking a reconstruction of a state government for Louisiana. When the message of 1863, with the plan before mentioned, reached New Orleans, Gen. Banks wrote me that he was confident the people, with his military cooperation, would reconstruct substantially on that plan. I wrote him and some of them to try it; they tried it, and the result is known. Such only has been my agency in getting up the Louisiana government. As to sustaining it, my promise is out, as before stated. But, as bad promises are better broken than kept, I shall treat this as a bad promise and break it whenever I shall be convinced that keeping it is adverse to the public interest. But I have not yet been so convinced.

I have been shown a letter on this subject, supposed to be an able one, in which the writer expresses regret that my mind has not seemed to be definitely fixed on the question whether the seceded states, so-called, are in the union or out of it. It would perhaps add astonishment to his regret were he to learn that since I have found professed union men endeavoring to make that question, I have purposely forborne any public expression upon it. As appears to me that question has not been, nor yet is, a practically material one, and that any discussion of it while it thus remains practically immaterial could have no effect other than the mischievous one of dividing our friends. As yet, whatever it may hereafter become, that question is bad as the basis of a controversy and good for nothing at all—a merely pernicious abstraction.

We all agree that the seceded states, so-called, are out of their proper practical relation with the union, and that the sole object of the government, civil and military, in regard to those states is to again get them into that proper practical relation. I believe it is not only possible but in fact easier to do this without deciding or even considering whether these states have even been out of the union than with it. Finding themselves safely at home, it would be utterly immaterial whether they had ever been abroad. Let us all join in doing the acts necessary to restoring the proper practical relations between these states and the union, and each forever after innocently indulge his own opinion whether, in doing the acts, he brought the states from without into the union or only gave them proper assistance, they never having been out of it.

The amount of constituency, so to ... speak, on which the new Louisiana government rests would be more satisfactory to all if it contained fifty, thirty, or even twenty thousand, instead of only about twelve thousand, as it does. It is also unsatisfactory to some that the elective franchise is not given to the colored man. I would myself prefer that it were now conferred on the very intelligent and on those who serve our cause as soldiers. Still the question is not whether the Louisiana government, as it stands, is quite all that is desirable. The question is, "Will it be wiser to take it as it is and help to improve it; or to reject and disperse it?" "Can Louisiana be brought into proper practical relation with the union sooner by sustaining or by discarding her new state government?"

Some twelve thousand voters in the heretofore slave state of Louisiana have sworn allegiance to the union, assumed to be the rightful political power of the state, held elections, organized a state government, adopted a Free State constitution giving the benefit of public schools equally to black and white, and empowering the legislature to confer the elective franchise upon the colored man. Their legislature has already voted to ratify the constitutional amendment recently passed by Congress abolishing slavery throughout the nation. These twelve thousand persons are thus fully committed to the union and to perpetual freedom in the state—committed to the very things and nearly all the things the nation wants—and they ask the nation's recognition and its assistance to make good their committal. Now, if we reject and spurn them, we do our utmost to disorganize and disperse them. We in effect say to the white men, "You are worthless, or worse—we will neither help you nor be helped by you." To the blacks we say, "This cup of liberty which these, your old masters, hold to your lips, we will dash from you and leave you to the chances of gathering the spilled and scattered contents in some vague and undefined when, where, and how." If this course, discouraging and paralyzing both white and black, has any tendency to bring Louisiana into proper practical relations with the union, I have so far been unable to perceive it. If, on the contrary, we recognize and sustain the new government of Louisiana, the converse of all this is made true. We encourage the hearts and nerve the arms of the twelve thousand to adhere to their work, and argue for it, and proselyte for it, and fight for it, and feed it, and grow it, and ripen it to a complete success. The colored man too, in seeing all united for him, is inspired with vigilance and energy and daring to the same end. Grant that he desires the elective franchise, will he not attain it sooner by saving the already advanced steps toward it than by running backward over them? Concede that the new government of Louisiana is only to what it should be as the egg is to the fowl, we shall sooner have the fowl by hatching the egg than by smashing it? Again, if we reject Louisiana, we also reject one vote in favor of the proposed amendment to the national Constitution. To meet this proposition, it has been argued that no more than three-fourths of those states which have not attempted secession are necessary to validly ratify the amendment. I do not commit myself against this further than to say that such a ratification would be questionable and sure to be persistently questioned, while a ratification by three-fourths of all the states would be unquestioned and unquestionable.

I repeat the question. "Can Louisiana be brought into proper practical relation with the union sooner by sustaining or by discarding her new state government?

What has been said of Louisiana will apply generally to other states. And yet so great peculiarities pertain to each state, and such important and sudden changes occur in the same state, and, withal, so new and unprecedented is the whole case, that no exclusive and inflexible plan can safely be prescribed as to details and collaterals. Such exclusive and inflexible plan would surely become a new entanglement. Important principles may, and must, be inflexible.

In the present "situation," as the phrase goes, it may be my duty to make some new announcement to the people of the South. I am considering and shall not fail to act when satisfied that action will be proper.

One man in this audience understood perfectly what Lincoln intimated. John Wilkes Booth told his companion, "That means nigger citizenship. Now, by God, I'll put him through. That is the last speech he will ever make." And indeed, the assassin struck a blow from which America has never recovered. The North lost a hero. African Americans lost an ally for fair and equal opportunity. The South lost a leader, Southern-born, who called for charity without malice. By murdering the president, on Good Friday no less, Booth guaranteed Father Abraham's place in history as a beloved martyr for freedom.

The issues Lincoln faced continue to have an impact today. Moral choice, democratic citizenship, and equality still mingle, and these essential words of Lincoln still inspire.

An officer of the Congressional National Abraham Lincoln Bicentennial Commission Foundation, Orville Vernon Burton is a prolific author and scholar. His most recent work is *The Age of Lincoln*, which won the *Chicago Tribune* Heartland Literary Award for Nonfiction and was selected for the Book of the Month Club, the History Book Club, and the Military Book Club. Burton is the Burroughs Professor of Southern History and Culture at Coastal Carolina University and is executive director of the College of Charleston's Program in the Carolina Lowcountry and Atlantic World. He was the founding director of the Institute for Computing in the Humanities, Arts, and Social Science (ICHASS) at the University of Illinois, where he is Emeritus University Distinguished Teacher/ Scholar and Professor of History, African American Studies, and Sociology. He and his wife, Georganne, live in Ninety Six, South Carolina. Visit his website at www.ageoflincoln.com.